Improving Schools in Difficulty

Improving Schools in Difficulty

Edited by
Paul Clarke

continuum
LONDON • NEW YORK

Continuum International Publishing Group
The Tower Building   15 East 26th Street
11 York Road   New York
London SE1 7NX   NY 10010

www.continuumbooks.com

British Library Cataloguing-in-Publication Data
A catalogue record for this book is available from the British Library.

ISBN: 0–8264–6473–4 (hardback)
       0–8264–6474–2 (paperback)

Typeset by Fakenham Photosetting Limited, Fakenham, Norfolk
Printed and bound in Great Britain by Antony Rowe, Chippenham, Wiltshire

Contents

In memory of my father
Gerry Clarke 1939–2002

Contributors

Mel Ainscow is Professor of Education, School of Education, University of Manchester.

Christopher Chapman is a research fellow at the University of Warwick Institute of Education.

Paul Clarke is Director of the Improving the Quality of Education for All (IQEA) programme.

John Gray is Professor of Education and Dean of Research at the Faculty of Education, University of Cambridge.

Alma Harris is Director of the Warwick Institute of Education.

John MacBeath is Professor of Educational Leadership at the University of Cambridge.

Daniel Muijs is Professor of Education at University of Newcastle upon Tyne where he works as a lecturer in Quantitative Research Methods.

Maria Nicolaidou has recently completed her PhD and is a teacher in Cyprus.

David Reynolds is Professor of Leadership and School Effectiveness at the University of Exeter.

Richard Riddell is a visiting fellow in the Faculty of Education at the University of the West of England and a former LEA Director of Education.

Jennifer Russ is a tutor at the University of Cambridge Institute of Education

Louise Stoll is Professor of Education at the University of Bath.

Mel West is Dean and Professor of Educational Leadership, University of Manchester.

Terry Wrigley is a lecturer in education at the University of Edinburgh.

Series Editors' Introduction

The challenge of improving schools in the most disadvantaged contexts is currently high on the political agenda. The school improvement evidence base points towards the difficulties disadvantaged schools face in simply getting to the starting line for improvement (e.g., Maden, 2001; Reynolds *et al.*, 2004; Myers and Stoll, 1998). High staff turnover, poor facilities, lack of resources, falling pupil numbers and a constant stream of supply teachers are pressures that schools in more prosperous areas simply do not face (Whitty, 2001). Initiatives such as Excellence in Cities (EiC) and Education Action Zones (EAZs) aimed at supporting schools in disadvantaged areas have had some success and there is recent evidence to suggest that targeted programmes of support and staff development can make a difference in the most disadvantaged school contexts (Reynolds *et al.*, 2004). The research evidence suggests that while the powerful effect of the socio-economic conditions cannot be ignored, the fact remains that schools can improve, despite their context or circumstances. Evidence shows that schools in challenging circumstances are able improve levels of student performance and achievement but that any improvement efforts may be short lived because of the vulnerability of their situation (Borman *et al.*, 2000; Harris *et al.*, 2003). In short, it is possible to improve schools in challenging circumstances but that it is more difficult remains unquestionable (Gray, 2001).

Although there are some studies of improving schools in disadvantaged areas, the empirical base remains relatively thin (Muijs *et al.*, 2004). Until relatively recently, the school effectiveness and school improvement research fields have not concentrated their substantial research efforts upon schools in difficult or challenging contexts. As Gray (2001: 33) concedes: 'we don't really know how much more difficult it is for schools serving disadvantaged communities to improve because much of the improvement research has ignored this dimension'. The reason for this lack of attention, it is suggested, resides predominantly in the inherent complexity and volatility of the terrain along with the difficulty of disaggregating the causal effects upon school performance and improvement. It is clear that more research is needed that explores not only how schools in challenging contexts improve but also how they sustain improvement over time.

Consequently, this book edited by Paul Clarke is both timely and important. It brings together leading researchers to provide contemporary perspectives on improving schools in difficulty. The contributions range from overviews of the literature to empirically grounded analyses and to in-depth case studies that illuminate the problems facing schools in difficult contexts. This is a rich and powerful combination of chapters, each taking a different perspective on improving schools in difficulty while simultaneously respecting the challenges facing these schools on a daily basis. There are many themes emerging from this book that will assist and inform researchers, practitioners and policy-makers. One theme that stands out is the need for highly differentiated and context-specific approaches to school improvement instead of wholesale, standardized solutions that ignore the powerful socio-economic factors that inevitably influence a school's ability to improve.

School improvement is a complex undertaking in any school but for schools in challenging circumstances, it presents extra difficulties. The core message about improving schools facing difficult or challenging circumstances is one of building capacity through empowering, involving and developing those within the school and by reducing external accountability and control. Increasing external scrutiny, intervention and pressure upon schools facing challenging circumstances are strategies that are least likely to bring about improvement in the long term. As Elmore (2003: 14) points out, to meet performance targets 'schools must develop successively higher capacities' and this can be achieved by generating internal accountability rather than responding to external accountability. It is clear that many accountability systems require schools with the lowest capacity to improve most through a combination of compliance and sanctions. Long term, this strategy is destined to fail unless capacity-building measures are simultaneously put in place.

We undoubtedly need to know much more about improving schools in difficult circumstances and particularly how such schools sustain improvement over time. We need to know what particular combinations of external support and internal development are optimum for generating positive change and development. Increasingly, the evidence base is pointing towards the possibilities and potential of 'learning communities' to generate the capacity for school improvement (Hargreaves, 2003). Such communities offer opportunities for teachers to work together without being dependent upon external initiatives or interventions. However, much depends upon a school's internal capacity to become a learning community in the first place. Gray (2004: 306) has pointed out that schools that create the capacity for improvement move through three phases of school improvement – 'catching up, consolidation and moving ahead'. He notes, however, that our ignorance about their 'starting points' serves as a block to improvement and suggests that 'we tend not to see these schools accurately because our frameworks are too limited'. The chapters in this book collectively present a powerful framework for 'seeing' schools in difficult contexts and for analysing their different capacities to improve. The book offers a starting point for unlocking the dynamics of the improvement process within schools in difficult contexts and, more importantly, acknowledges and respects the contribution of those teachers who continue to work there.

Alma Harris
Jane McGregor
Series Editors

References

Borman, G. D., Rachuba, L., Datnow, A., Alberg, M., Maciver, M. and Stringfield, S. (2000) *Four Models of School Improvement. Successes and Challenges in Reforming Low-Performing, High Poverty Title 1 Schools*. Baltimore: Johns Hopkins University, Center for Research into the Education of Students Placed at Risk.

Elmore, R. (2003) *Knowing the Right Thing to Do: School Improvement and Performance-Based Accountability:* Best Practices Center, NGA, Harvard University.

Gray, J. (2001) Introduction in *Success Against the Odds: Five Years On*. London: Routledge.

Gray, J. (2004) 'Frames of reference and traditions of interpretation: some issues in the identification of "under-achieving" schools', *British Journal of Educational Studies*, 52, 3, 293–309.

Hargreaves, A. (2003) *Teaching in the Knowledge Society: Education in an Age of Insecurity*. Buckingham: Open University Press.

Harris, A., Muijs, D., Chapman, C., Stoll, L. and Russ, J. (2003) *Raising Attainment in Former Coalfield Areas*. Sheffield: Department for Education and Skills.

Maden, M. (ed.) (2001) *Success Against the Odds: Five Years On*. London: Routledge.

Myers, K. and Stoll, L. (1998) *No Quick Fixes: Improving Schools in Difficulty*. London, Falmer Press.

Muijs, D., Harris, A., Chapman, C., Stoll, L. and Russ, J. (2004) 'Improving schools in socio-economically disadvantaged areas: a review of the research evidence', *International Journal of School Effectiveness and School Improvement*, 15, 2, 149–75.

Reynolds, D., Clarke, P. and Harris, A. (2004) 'Improving schools in exceptionally challenging circumstances', *American Education Research Association Conference*, 11–16 April, San Diego.

Whitty, G. (2001) 'Education, social class and social exclusion', *Education & Social Justice*, 1, 1, 2–8.

Preface

This book seeks to explore the troubled ground of improving schools in difficulty.

Troubled ground? Well, for the last few years we have seen wave after wave of reform aimed at improving the lot of the school struggling at the bottom of the ladder of performance and, despite what can be interpreted as best intentions, the problem persists. As a social problem it draws down significant sums of public money, it exercises many talented people and yet, time after time, we find that three, four, maybe five years down the road after extended efforts the impact of the work diffuses and the challenges remain, doggedly evident in people's daily lives. It suggests that perhaps something is wrong in our interpretation, in our analysis, in our approach and in our consequent measure of effect of our activity with difficult schools.

Troubled ground, because in asking provocative questions about the principles of development, the priorities identified and the strategies and the interpretations used to make improvements, one inevitably encroaches upon the hard work and effort that other colleagues have applied to the problem. Asking questions, and not taking the existing assertions for granted, is always going to put one into difficult situations, particularly when many people have been committed to a strategic approach and have invested their careers and personal integrity to a set of solutions. However, I have always believed that to be most useful, research should be deliberately provocative, probing and challenging assumptions in the search for deeper understanding and new ways of formulating approaches to tired solutions. A system which fails to engage with objection and challenge is not a learning system; we teeter on the edge of systemic intolerance at this time. Where there is a centralized assertion that the primary function of education is to ensure economic competitiveness, there is a grave danger of utilitarianism becoming the primary driver of the school. This is at once both particularly true in required practice and poignantly problematic in social significance in schools facing difficult social and economic circumstance, where the false premise of economic salvation is often used as the basis for educational reform.

In the spirit of shared learning, a number of colleagues who regularly work in and with schools in difficulty have generously agreed to share their current thinking on different aspects of their work in this book. The book is very much a work in progress: we each share an ongoing interest in schools in difficulty and the chapters fashioned here capture only a small part of that wider body of work.

In making sense of my colleagues contributions and in clarifying my own feelings and thoughts about this work I have tried to create something of a story. It is a story that uses ideas and reflections as a guide to some of the challenges that we collectively grapple with as we work in this difficult field. At the same time I would hope that the book offers you as a reader a chance to frame your own reflections on what is perhaps the most pressing area of attention in education at this time: that of redefining the purpose of the school, not just for those schools deemed to be working in difficult circumstances, but also for the wider community of schools. By focusing on one domain of schools, it is possible sometimes to widen the horizon and to expose some deeper themes which pertain to a bigger debate. I think that the contributions herein offer just such possibilities and provide a set of insights which can lead to further discussion and action.

The book is structured around two parts: part one examines the principles of engagement with schools in difficulty and part two looks at ways of improving the process of supporting schools in difficulty. It seems to me that what we are saying collectively suggests that a new line of interpretation of challenge is emerging which is far more critical of the existing arrangements, taking a view of improvement which is more deeply rooted into the emancipatory potential of education as a vehicle for social change.

Our views are not impractical or simply theoretical, they are rooted in practice and arise from observation of practice, they remain discontented with the dominant discourse of change and they make a call for more radical solutions to be exercised. This is an important theme, it matters to us all, as students, as parents, as teachers and as citizens that we ensure that all our people have the greatest possible opportunities to succeed and flourish in their lives as creative individuals living inside dynamic supportive communities. It is imperative that we all participate in this endeavour; it is not the domain of an elite few. I recall a recent conversation with a parent and a teacher as we chatted over ways of tackling pupil underachievement, 'Our kids recognize that what we have at present is just not good enough, and that they have a very big part to play in changing the way that we do school – the trouble is they don't as yet have a voice in that debate.'

PAUL CLARKE

Frontpiece: A Matter of Definition

Paul Clarke

Words define worlds
Wittgenstein

What do we mean by 'Improving schools in difficulty: principle and process' and in particular what is meant by difficulty? At first glance the title suggests a 'how to' book: how to go in and do things in a school for the betterment of those working there. Whilst we explore some ways we have worked with colleagues in school, it is not the case that we are suggesting the imposition from outside of particular methods of working, indeed our epistemology is quite different. Instead, we are trying to expose some of the challenges faced by such schools and to examine ways in which strategic approaches have been devised that seek to improve them. Therefore the 'principle' is concerned closely with a way of engaging with school colleagues as a collective effort, where school improvement is undertaken *with* staff and not *done to* staff. The 'process' of that improvement is to build upon emergent knowledge – that is, knowledge arising from working in schools facing difficult circumstances. The contributors to this book, in various ways, are suggesting that whilst there may be a general consensus that something should be done to enable schools in difficulty to improve, the nature and mechanism of that improvement remains highly contested and is, as yet, by no means clearly defined. The contributions here pointedly suggest that in order to make sense of the 'improvement' we need first to examine the thinking that exists behind the labels that we are using when describing educational challenge of this sort.

'Difficulty', 'challenging circumstances' and 'exceptionally challenging circumstances' are the current labels most regularly used to describe a discrete set of schools working within a society in a process of transition in environments which differ markedly from what might be accepted as tolerable. The individual labels matter little, but what does matter is the lived experience of people who find themselves located, for whatever reason, within organizations and communities deemed to be in the category of challenge. For there is a reality beyond the rhetoric of policy, a reality of struggle, often connected with poverty, that lies at their core. At the time of writing, the main news item informs listeners that the gap between the rich and poor in Britain has increased fivefold since the coming to power of New Labour. The characteristic tendency to point to the fault of the local institution and local actors whilst failing to consider the broader economic consequences of policy which fails to redistribute wealth is, and has been, a dominant feature of the New Labour approach. Clearly the motivational possibility of education becomes more of a likelihood in circumstances where people can see the gains both personally and for their immediate friends and families. From such starting points comes sustainable commitments to learning, but it will not come without a real sense of fairness and equity, and many of the communities in which we find schools in difficulty are located in truly desperate places, where both national and local policy has failed to tackle a slow economic decline, generation after generation.

When we describe schools in difficulty, we run the danger of generalizing beyond what should be our primary locus of attention – the focus on the person. It is a real danger and the educational road is littered with the old carcasses of failed reform which should remind us every way we turn of the persistent problem of failed intervention and false diagnosis (Sarason, 1990). We need to be reminded that as we generalize we correspondingly find ourselves moving away from the particular need. These needs are closely associated to a particular set of locally lived circumstances, they are 'context specific' to use the jargon. The trouble is that if one is content to see the world in this generalized way, it then becomes possible to generate blanket definitions, which often lead to blanket solutions, which in turn become the basis of funding and intervention.

It seems to be the case, after more than twenty years of predominantly external educational reform in England, that even the most powerful and persuasively phrased policy introduced with integrity and commitment still appears to users to be a solution generated from outside. Such policy is perceived by teachers as something that is done to them, rather than done with them. As a result it is viewed with suspicion and very often with resistance. What is clear is that policy can only mandate technicalities, it cannot define cultures and as such it lacks a critical dimension: that of engagement of those with whom the problem is a lived experience in a specific context. Distance from definition, and in this case from policy formation, permits individual disengagement, whereas closeness to definition demands personal connection. It is also diagnosed in isolation and, despite much rhetoric of 'joined-up thinking' (I prefer to suggest that what is meant in grown-up terms is 'integrated thinking'), the reality remains that schools are expected to go it alone. The new initiatives such as leadership incentive grants offer the possibility for inter-school and possibly even inter-agency development, but in reality there often remains a lack of will at local authority level to do this, possibly because it undermines their existing power base, and the continuing problem posed by performance league tables means that any inter-school development is at best running counter to other parts of the policy programme and are viewed with suspicion.

One feature of working with schools in difficulty might, therefore, be to personalize the action, to localize the challenge and to engage and empower the actors – in this case teaching staff – to connect with the problems that they define as challenging, rather than giving them a pre-existing definition of challenge. But here comes the rub, and it connects to the second theme of this book, the matter of process – how to 'think' about how to 'do' the improvement.

The dominant method of engaging staff in reform remains externally and not internally led interpretation and diagnosis of challenge. In fact, experience suggests that when this is turned on its head and the person closest to the problem of challenge defines the challenge, the staff and students are more engaged. This observation causes untold problems when faced with multi-site reform arising from central policy. Instead of a 'roll out' mentality, where replicable strategies are placed in front of many, similarly defined schools, it may be time to rethink the definition and then to differentiate the processes. Through challenging the definition of challenge, we start to ask deeper questions about the nature of localized need and, in turn, we are reminded that to make sense of that need it is imperative that we enter into more constructive dialogue with those people most closely affected by it.

What I am suggesting is that the definition of challenge itself should be challenged, because it assumes meaning and asserts control over situations which may prove to be false and it reifies the dominant methodological view in educational reform that external expertise and insight is the mainstay of meaningful and sustainable reform. It seems timely, therefore, to question and consider whether there are other ways of understanding challenge, other ways of responding to it and other ways of constructing strategic alliances which take full advantage of localized understanding whilst at the same time connecting those localized understandings to a wider resource of knowledge and insight.

This book takes on that theme of describing and then examining in detail the ways in which schools in difficulty are being supported. Our diagnosis of the difficulty is not necessarily common, as we can see in the different ways that difficulty is interpreted. We offer this to you for further reflection, analysis and discussion.

Reference

Sarason, S. (1990) *The Predictable Failure of Educational Reform: Can We Change Course Before It's Too Late?* San Francisco: Jossey-Bass.

Part One
Schools in Difficulty: A Matter of Principle

1 Challenging the Challenged: Developing an Improvement Programme for Schools Facing Extremely Challenging Circumstances

Paul Clarke, David Reynolds and Alma Harris

CHAPTER OVERVIEW

This chapter outlines a contemporary research and development programme that focused on a group of eight secondary schools in England. The schools in this study were considered to be facing extremely challenging circumstances primarily reflected in high levels of socio-economic disadvantage that impacted upon them. They were also schools considered to be seriously under-performing and in need of particular improvement and support strategies. The chapter outlines the background, nature and scope of the improvement programme designed for this group of schools, collectively known as the 'Octet' group. It reflects upon the progress that has been made and, more significantly, the lessons emerging about the limitations and possibilities of improving schools in the most difficult circumstances.

Introduction

The educational reform agenda in many countries reflects urgent attention to the issue of improving schools in the most difficult or disadvantaged circumstances. The issue of 'underachievement' is high on the political agenda in the USA, Canada and England as it remains clear that certain groups of pupils in schools in disadvantaged contexts consistently fail to reach their potential while other groups of pupils in more affluent contexts consistently succeed. Recent research has shown that children from low income families do not on average overcome the hurdle of lower initial attainment. It also highlights that class differences affect children long before they start school and have a growing influence as they get older. The odds, it would seem, are 'still stacked against schools in poorer areas' and the social class differential remains a powerful indicator of subsequent educational achievement.

Although it cannot be denied that there is a strong negative correlation between most measures of social disadvantage and school achievement, some schools facing difficult and challenging circumstances *are* able to add significant value to levels of pupil achievement and learning. There is evidence to suggest that certain schools do improve despite high levels of disadvantage. However, the evidence also shows that such schools have to exceed 'normal' efforts to secure this improvement. In summary, these schools have to work much harder at sustaining performance levels than schools in more privileged areas and they have to maintain that effort 'as success can be short-lived and fragile in difficult or challenging circumstances'.

In addition, schools in disadvantaged areas face a myriad of problems in simply getting to the starting line for improvement. High staff turnover, poor facilities, lack of resources, falling pupil numbers and a constant stream of supply teachers are pressures that schools in more prosperous areas simply do not face. Research has also shown that factors such as geographical isolation – particularly of rural schools – selective local educational systems, weak support from some Local Education Authorities (LEAs), low levels of formal qualifications in the local adult population and poor employment opportunities further compound the problem and make the extent of the educational challenge facing these schools significantly greater than schools in more favourable settings (Reynolds *et al.*, 2001).

The net result of this amalgam of social and economic problems means it is inevitably more difficult to improve schools in challenging contexts because of the complex set of variables affecting each one. Study after study has reinforced the fact that social background factors (SES) explain more than half the variation in pupil achievement and illustrate how SES is related to other important factors such as staying on rates, adult employment and crime. Yet, improving schools and raising standards of achievement in disadvantaged areas remains both an aspiration and an expectation. It is clear that 'improving against the odds is now the name of the game' irrespective of socio-economic context or degrees of disadvantage.

In England, the improvement of the lowest attaining schools remains high on the government's reform agenda. Despite concerted attempts to tackle this particular problem there remains an urgent need to secure ways of raising student achievement in schools located in areas of higher than average socio-economic deprivation. Since 2001 a wide range of work has been undertaken with the chief aim of assisting schools in challenging circumstances to improve. Initially, this work was conceptual and theory forming and resulted in:

- the generation of a conceptual review that sought to locate the present state of school improvement so that work could be conceptually up to date (Hopkins and Reynolds, 2001);
- the generation of literature reviews about the school development planning process (Hopkins *et al.*, 2001) and the implications of research in school effectiveness and school improvement for what schools could do to improve themselves (Reynolds *et al.*, 2001);
- a series of seminars and meetings for the headteachers and other senior managers in the schools, designed to both update them with knowledge about 'what might work' and provide systems of mutual support that would help generate increased 'educational resilience' in practitioners exposed to multiple stresses.

In the last three or four years a concerted effort has been made to raise the performance of 'schools facing challenging circumstances' (SFCC) through a combination of increased resources, various developmental programmes and targeted professional development opportunities. Also, specific funding and alternative approaches to improvement have emerged intended specifically to assist schools in difficult circumstances. Initiatives like 'Excellence in Cities', Educational Action Zones and, most recently, the London Challenge and the Leadership Incentive Grant have all targeted schools in areas of disadvantage or 'challenging circumstances'.

The Octet Project: third-wave school improvement

In 2001, a research and development project was commissioned by the DfES with the prime purpose of working with a group of eight schools located in the greatest 'category' of challenge in the English education system, i.e., 'schools facing extremely challenging circumstances' (SfECC). Put simply, these schools were located in communities which face some of the most difficult economic and social challenges with associated challenges of poverty including poor housing and poor social welfare, and difficult inter-cultural relations. The aim of the project was to work with eight secondary schools over a two to three year timescale to generate an intensive programme of intervention that could potentially be replicated in other schools facing 'extreme challenges'. This project became known as the 'Octet Project' and as a team we were commissioned to work with these schools to mutually develop and trial a specifically tailored school improvement for the eight schools.

Our theoretical and practical stance on school improvement was consistent with what Reynolds and Hopkins (2002) have termed 'third-wave' school improvement. This third phase directly influenced our design and subsequent development work with the Octet schools. These three phases of school improvement will now be briefly summarized.

- The first phase was epitomized by the OECD's *International School Improvement Project* (ISIP) (Hopkins, 1987) but unfortunately many of the initiatives associated with this first phase of school improvement were 'free floating', rather than representing a systematic, programmatic and coherent approach to school change. There was correspondingly, in this phase, an emphasis upon organizational change, school self-evaluation and the 'ownership of change' by individual schools and teachers, but these initiatives were loosely connected to student learning outcomes, both conceptually and practically, were variable and fragmented in conception and application and, consequently, in the eyes of most school improvers the practices struggled to impact upon classroom practice (Hopkins, 2001; Reynolds, 1999).

- The second phase of development began in the early 1990s and resulted from the interaction between the school improvement and the school effectiveness communities. In these years the school improvement tradition was beginning to provide schools with guidelines and strategies for implementation that were sufficiently powerful to begin to take educational change into classrooms. Approaches to staff development based upon partnership teaching (Joyce and Showers, 1995), and designs for development planning that focused upon learning outcomes and which linked together organizational and classroom change within a medium-term time frame (Hopkins and MacGilchrist, 1998) are but two examples of the school improvement contribution. Fullan (1991) provides a useful survey of the first two ages of this school improvement enterprise.

- The third phase of school improvement developed from the somewhat uncomfortable evidence that the wide range of national educational reforms produced in various countries, and the contributions of the school improvement communities of many countries additionally, may not have been particularly successful. Despite the dramatic increase in education reform efforts in most countries, their impact upon overall levels of student achievement are widely seen as not having been as successful as anticipated. Although there may have been pockets of relatively short-lived success in certain countries, such as the National Literacy and Numeracy strategies in

England (Fullan, 2000), and individual programmes which appear to be effective over time, such as *Success for All* (Slavin, 1996), the evidence from major programmes such as 'New American Schools' is the limitation of 'off the shelf' improvement or 'whole school designs' to secure long-term and widespread system and school improvement.

Consequently, third age or phase school improvement attempts to draw from the lessons of previous and existing improvement and reform. It is in evidence in a number of improvement programmes in England, such as the Improving the Quality of Education for All (IQEA) Project, the High Reliability Schools (HRS) Project and many of the projects associated with the London Institute of Education National School Improvement Network (NSIN). In Canada, it has been in evidence in the various phases of work conducted in the Halton Board of Education in Ontario and the highly influential Manitoba School Improvement Project. In the Netherlands, it has been in evidence in the Dutch National School Improvement Project (further details on all these programmes can be located in Reynolds *et al.,* 1996; Teddlie and Reynolds, 2000; Hopkins *et al.,* 1994; Hopkins, 2001; Harris and Young, 2000).

There are, of course, course variations *between* these various programmes that make any global assessment difficult. Nevertheless, if one were to compare these examples of third-wave school improvement *as a group* it is clear that:

- There has been an enhanced focus upon the importance of *pupil outcomes*. Instead of the earlier emphasis upon changing the processes of schools, the focus is now upon seeing if these changes are powerful enough to affect pupil outcomes.
- The learning level and the *instructional* behaviours of teachers have been increasingly targeted for explicit attention, rather than the school level.
- There has been the creation of an infrastructure to enable the knowledge base, both 'best practice' and research findings, to be utilized. This has involved an internal focus on collaborative patterns of staff development that enable teachers to enquire into practice, and external strategies for dissemination and networking.
- There has been an increasing consciousness of the importance of 'capacity building'. This includes not only staff development, but also medium-term strategic planning, change strategies that utilize 'pressure and support', as well as the intelligent use of external support agencies.

- There has been an adoption of a 'mixed' *methodological orientation*, in which bodies of quantitative data plus qualitative data are used to measure quality and variation in that quality. This includes an audit of existing classroom and school processes and outcomes, and comparison with desired end states, in particular the educational experiences of different pupil groups.
- There has been an increased emphasis upon the importance of ensuring reliability or 'fidelity' in programme implementation across all organizational members within schools, a marked contrast with the past when improvement programmes did not have to be organizationally 'tight'.
- There has been an appreciation of the importance of *cultural change* in order to embed and sustain school improvement. There has been a focus on a careful balance between 'vision building' and the adapting of structures to support those aspirations.
- There has also been an increased concern to ensure that the improvement programmes relate to, and impact upon, practitioners and practices through using increasingly sophisticated training, coaching and development programmes.

These third-phase practices and philosophies of school improvement (more fully described in Hopkins, 2001) provided the conceptual and practical framework for our work with the eight schools facing extremely challenging circumstances. The remainder of this chapter describes this process and reflects upon progress to date.

Early stages of programme design

There were three key factors that needed to be taken into consideration prior to thinking about programme design. The first was the specific variable nature of 'extreme challenge' as the challenges facing the eight schools were far from uniform. This meant that the team had to account in the design of the programme for the nuances of local school need and allow for the possibility for school-level interpretation, redesign and integration into planned and ongoing activity. Second, there was an inherent sensitivity to the label 'extremely challenging circumstances'. We were acutely aware that this labelling could be construed negatively by the eight schools, which were already under the microscope in terms of their performance and accountability. Hence, we were clear that the design of the programme was not remedial in intention but was intended to be at the cutting edge of knowledge about third-wave improvement.

Third, there was a danger of developing a 'one-size-fits-all' programme and indeed some early external pressure to do so. Consequently, the team needed to be certain that the programme could deliver a core of necessary elements of activity but with elements that could ensure site-by-site variation in adoption and adaptation.

1 Finding common ground

Our discussion on the early formulation of the strategy for the programme led us to a series of three rather nervous discussions with the eight headteachers from the schools. Nervous because we didn't know them and they didn't know us, and because we had been appointed by the DfES, a powerful external authority and their suspicion as a group of headteachers was that we would force a strategy upon them and their schools. These early discussions served the purpose of clarifying ways of working and smoothed out the concerns which were being voiced. However, it would be fair to say that it would not be until after the second full seminar session with the school teams that the suspicions about the exact nature of our role and about our ways of working with the schools would be more assured.

2 Clarifying process and principles

Early discussions with the headteachers also identified that the programme was seen by the schools as a means of experimenting with established knowledge bases, with a view to opening up a series of investigations into ways of enhancing school by school the capacity to introduce and maintain new approaches to learning which challenged students and enthused and engaged staff. Our initial face-to-face planning only allowed time for three meetings with headteachers; after each meeting they returned to their schools and consulted with their own staff. This was difficult because we had no opportunity to meet with the teachers with whom we would be working until the first full seminar programme. However, the channel of discussion between the heads, their colleagues in school and ourselves generated a number of shared issues of principle and presented us with an emergent way of working.

It was agreed that both schools and programme team wanted to:

- establish a way of working with the schools which was conducive to experimentation;
- explore and improvise with innovative approaches to teaching and in the support of learning;
- deepen the competence of the school-based teams through very deliberate strategies which would encourage collegial practice;

- explore ways of taking advantage of the inter-school dimension of the programme by encouraging the reporting of findings and sharing of school-based experiences with colleagues from other school sites involved in the programme.

It was also agreed that the programme would comprise 'tight' and 'loose' components. The 'tight' components were the focus on data to highlight areas for change, attention to the instructional processes, attention to the emotional or affective domain and, lastly, a requirement of inter-school sharing, i.e., the power of eight. The programme was designed in process terms in a way that allowed for choice and differentiation across different school sites. The 'loose' components aligned with the ways of working adopted by the school improvement group (SIG) and how the SIG chose to disseminate and activate key developments in teaching and learning within their own school context. In summary, the programme design encompassed two central dimensions: *a theory of instruction* based upon certain bodies of knowledge about effective teaching and models of teaching; and a *theory of practice* based upon the theory of action learning and action research principles.

3 Generating a programme design

The initial discussions with headteachers established a basic consensus about the intentions, components and core expectations of the programme. We reflected carefully as a team on the related matters of programme style, programme content, programme methodology and the forms of school-based follow-up by the teachers and through our own school visits. The model of change that informed our thinking essentially was one that intended to move the schools from a position of relative dependency to independency to inter-dependency. The aim was to generate *learning communities* both within and across schools. As a catalyst to achieve this, each school was asked to establish SIG on the lines of the IQEA programme (see Hopkins *et al.*, 1999; Ainscow, *et al.*, 2004). Each school was encouraged to create a cross-sectional team which would provide a range of viewpoints from different perspectives in the school, extending from classroom teachers, to middle managers, to senior management colleagues.

The SIG provided the internal 'improvement' team and a direct link to schools through a named SIG coordinator. The intention was that the SIG would be the focus of training and development but that they would be agents of change within the school by actively disseminating and demonstrating new instructional practices. Regular discussion and meetings with a core team at training events as well as regular meetings with the SIG teams at their schools meant that the activist dimension of the SIG group was constantly reinforced. There was an expectation that they would influence, shape and inform the instructional practices within the school. The SIG groups also ensured that we were able to develop close and reciprocal links with colleagues in school enabling us to constantly re-align the programme to school-level needs.

Programme characteristics: promoting difference, strategy and integrity

Having defined a SIG group within each school with whom we were going to work, we needed to consider the way of working and what the focus of that work might take. We concluded that three clear issues were of value to us in the programme which reflected our ongoing discussions with headteachers and confirmed many of our own experiences.

The first theme was recognition of the importance of *difference.* These schools were all categorized as being in extremely challenging circumstances, yet they all had particular social and cultural nuances which set them apart uniquely from each other in terms of experience and approach. The challenge for us was to develop a sufficiently differentiated and flexible programme model which would provide each school with a conceptual shape within which to work but, at the same time, allow school colleagues to fashion their own approach based on their identification of their own localized need.

The second theme was concerned with *teaching or instruction.* We noted that there was a necessity to attend to both management and classroom conditions if we were to have any long-term likelihood of impact and effect. If we were to have impact, our design therefore had to capture the interest of the classroom teacher and extend into the management and leadership structures of the school. A common denominator seemed to be that of learning and teaching.

The third theme was concerned with ensuring programme *reliability, integrity or fidelity.* Drawing from our own experience, and from other reported school improvement initiatives, we believed that this was best achieved by our remaining close to the schools and by encouraging ownership. This necessitated a reciprocal approach, where school improvement groups were encouraged by programme leaders to identify their own themes for investigation and development and to bring these to the attention of the wider community of schools with whom we were working. To achieve this we pursued the idea of job-embedded staff development where coaching, mentoring, examination and reflection on student work and teaching practices, visiting other classrooms and other schools are all closely associated with needs identified by the individual teacher or her SIG.

Programme procedures

During the early stages of the programme we took the lead role in running workshops which SIGs were able to select according to interest. These workshops focused on instructional practice and the effective domain and this was a consistent pattern of provision throughout the training element of the programmes. The workshop materials provided a catalyst for discussion and subsequent school- and classroom-based development in each school. The insights gained from these training days prompted developmental work at each school that was subsequently shared with other schools in all remaining training sessions. At each training session each SIG had the opportunity to share, showcase and reflect upon their work. This was a deliberate strategy to move schools from dependency on the programme team to seeing themselves as mutually interdependent and part of a learning community of eight schools. At a deeper level, the deliberate transfer of responsibility to the SIGs to moderate and run sessions at every training event has provided an important forum for discussion and a collective resource which makes discussion about the change process more vibrant and more connected to their school setting.

Reflecting upon the programme

Over an 18-month period of involvement with these Octet schools we have learnt a great deal about the change process in schools in extremely challenging circumstance. The experience has highlighted the tensions and difficulties in building real learning communities within and across schools. Two tensions in particular seemed important:

- There was a genuine difficulty in schools actually getting going productively, that lasted about eight months. They could see the usefulness of concepts such as 'school learning communities' but were unsure of how to actually 'get there'! Once there was inter-change between schools, and teachers were able to see things being tried and working in other schools, then they began to use the programme to best effect.

- There was evidence that schools were pulled two different ways by the demands of 'maintenance' that emanated from inspection agencies and the need to 'develop' that was the programme remit. All schools had a range of demands to meet – from government, local authorities, local communities and local press which competed for scarce resources of time and emotion with the programme activities.

Our work has also brought into sharp relief the danger of labelling and reinforced the need to factor in emotions in the change process, which is often so neglected or ignored in contemporary approaches to change. Most importantly, it has highlighted the need to build a two-way dialogue into the fabric of a professional learning programme in order to secure and support classroom-based change. In summary, there are three main conclusions about working effectively with schools in extremely challenging circumstances. These are given below.

1 Using the right emotional tone

From the outset it was decided to treat the schools as any other set of schools and not to place too much emphasis upon the label 'extremely challenging circumstances' schools. From the outset it struck an invitational tone which the team sought to maintain throughout the life of the programme and which we feel our school colleagues have valued. The language used throughout was supportive and challenging rather than judgemental or critical. In retrospect, the label was not relevant to the implementation or developmental processes adopted by the schools. The programme was context specific insofar that all the schools were able to adopt and adapt what they learned to suit their school situation and local needs. There was a deliberate attempt to focus on school and classroom issues rather than attempt to deal with the wider socio-economic forces that adversely affected all eight schools.

2 A pedagogic and organizational focus

The programme deliberately incorporated a pedagogical or instructional focus in keeping with third-wave improvement. The aim of the programme was to generate and facilitate wider organizational change through concentrating primarily upon improving instructional effectiveness. This dual focus was intended to develop capacity building at the whole school and at the classroom level. This approach combined bodies of existing knowledge, including models of teaching, with the emerging findings of the school improvement groups themselves about instructional practices that were working successfully so far.

The resulting classroom impact has been significant, with each school improvement group reporting pedagogic changes which have been more inclusive, have been based on more active learning techniques and have resulted in higher student performance in all but one school in examination at Years 9 and 11. These changes have not been tied to classrooms however, the SIGs have led numerous staff training days and in four cases they now run the entire staff development scheme for the school. Structural changes have also been made to curriculum schedules, school day, meeting and planning times, team teaching and staff training.

3 Maximizing programme integrity

The regular two-day training events proved to be a vital factor in establishing successful working relationships and generating the knowledge base for development and change in schools. It has been significant because it has increased the opportunity for us to listen to what the schools are saying, rather than telling the schools what to think. It has established an expectation amongst participants where they now anticipate that there will be new additions to their resources at the end of the event which they can develop further in their own school settings, and it pushes the external team to consider carefully the leading issues that they feel are relevant to the event. This mutual responsibility has changed the experience of these types of events from one where the participants are passive recipients of knowledge, to one where they are actively engaged in presenting and challenging other colleagues' viewpoints.

Over their period of working with us they have talked together about aspirations for change, pursued specific activity inside their own schools, reflected on what has happened, reported this back to colleagues in the SIG and then to the wider network of SIGs in the programme, received critical feedback and modified their work accordingly and reinvested their findings into their own school settings through further investigation and training events with their teaching colleagues. The teachers have reported to us in the feedback data we have gathered that they now see a bigger picture of change than when they started and that they feel more confident that they can have an immediate effect on the direction of the change.

Reflections and commentary

We started the programme with the desire to offer practical help to eight schools that were facing extremely challenging circumstances, whilst at the same time advancing thinking about how the new 'third-wave' paradigm in school improvement could be put to the empirical test. The results from the first two years of the programme have been very encouraging, with seven out of eight schools improving their academic results, often by considerably more than the national rate of improvement of about a 1 per cent rise in the 'headline' figure of percentage of children gaining five or more higher grade passes at GCCE.[1]

What we are suggesting, then, is that the programme has opened up a very interesting design for facilitating professional learning which can be seen as two discrete domains of development operating as a double loop of learning. The first loop which we facilitate at the programme level is inter-school driven, the second loop is facilitated at the school level and is within school learning. The common link between the levels are the SIGs and their specific areas of development. The model originates from outside school but becomes locked into the internal school training cycle for professional learning (Clarke, 2000).

There are a number of issues that have emerged and are worth considering following the completion of the Octet Project in the summer of 2004. The first is one of *sustainability* after the resources, training, support and financial incentives have been removed. Research findings have clearly shown the vulnerability of resource-hungry initiatives in the long term and have pointed to the issue of sustaining activities once the external support and impetus is removed. The second related issue is that of *staff turnover*, which is already high in these schools but has proved to be particularly the case for those teachers involved in the Octet Project. One of the unintended consequences of equipping teachers with high-level instructional strategies means they become a very attractive proposition to other schools. The third issue is that of *scaling up*. The current obsession with scaling up in school reform is based on relatively few examples of success. It is questionable whether scaling up the Octet process is possible, realistic or even desirable. The intensive way of working with schools is both costly and relatively slow but there are elements of the programme like instructional and emotional training materials that could be distributed to other schools. However, without the associated resource, training and support it is unlikely that these materials will have a significant impact on schools that choose to use them.

Finally, there is the residing powerful issue of *external factors* that continue to impact negatively upon the school irrespective of its efforts to improve and sustain improvement. Critics of the school effectiveness and school improvement movement have consistently argued that unless the wider social and economic inequities are addressed, schools in challenging circumstances are unlikely to improve. They argue that those in the school improvement field are misguided and rather naïve if they think their efforts can make any difference against the socio-economic weight of disadvantage that grips schools and their wider communities.

They are right, of course, but only up to a point. While it is foolish to believe that individual schools can reverse the deep-rooted inequalities in society by their own efforts, it is equally perverse to ignore the fact that some schools are able to make a difference to the learning and lives of young people despite massive obstacles. If as West and Pennel (2003: 197) suggest, 'we should not be overly optimistic about solutions being readily found' to underachievement and social inequality, then, as we wait, surely it is better to try and seek some collective solutions, however short term, with those teachers who work in schools in the most difficult circumstances than to do absolutely nothing. The Octet Project was quite simply an attempt to work collaboratively with teachers in schools facing considerable and, in some cases insurmountable, difficulties and to develop new approaches to the teaching and learning issues they faced.

As the long-term pattern of inequality looks set to remain and as schools in challenging circumstances wait for politicians to set social policy to reverse their fate, they may be forgiven for developing their own strategies for improvement. While such strategies are unlikely to offset the macro effects of disadvantage, there is some evidence arising from within the Octet Project of positive influences upon teaching and learning. For this alone the work of these teachers in schools facing extremely challenging circumstances deserves to be recognized and celebrated.

Note

1 External examinations at 16.

References

Ainscow, M., Clarke, P. & West, M. (2004) *Frameworks for School Development*. Todmorden: IQEA Publications.
Clarke, P. (2000) *Learning Schools, Learning Systems*. London: Continuum.

Fullan, M. (1991) *The New Meaning of Educational Change*. London: Cassell.

Fullan, M. (2000) 'The return of large scale reform', in *The Journal of Educational Change*, 1, 1.

Gray, J., Reynolds, D., Fitz-Gibbon, C. & Jesson, D. (1996) *Merging Traditions: The Future of Research on School Effectiveness & School Improvement*. London: Cassell.

Harris, A. and Young, J. (2000) 'Comparing school improvement programmes in the United Kingdom and Canada: lessons learned'. *School Leadership and Management*. 20, 1, 31–43.

Hopkins, D. (ed.) (1987) *Improving the Quality of Schooling*. Lewes: Falmer Press.

Hopkins, D. (2001) *School Improvement for Real*. London: Falmer Press.

Hopkins, D., Ainscow, M. & West, M. (1994) *School Improvement in an Era of Change*. London: Cassell.

Hopkins, D. & MacGilchrist, B. (1998) 'Development planning for student achievement', in *School Leadership and Management*, 18, 3, 409–23.

Hopkins, D., *et al.* (2001) *Improving the Quality of Education for All*. London: David Fulton Publishers.

Hopkins, D. and Reynolds, D. (2001) 'The past, present and future of school improvement: towards the third age', in *British Educational Research Journal*, 27, 4, 459–75.

Joyce, B. & Showers, B. (1995) *Student Achievement Through Staff Development* (2nd edition). White Plains, NY: Longman.

Reynolds, D. (1999) 'School effectiveness, school improvement & contemporary educational policies', in J. Demaine (ed.) *Contemporary Educational Policy & Politics*. London: Macmillan, 65–81.

Reynolds, D., Hopkins, D. & Stoll, L. (1993) 'Linking school effectiveness knowledge and school improvement practice: towards a synergy', in *School Effectiveness and School Improvement*, 4, 1, 37–58.

Reynolds, D., Creemers, B. P. M., Hopkins, D., Stoll, L. & Bollen, R. (1996) *Making Good Schools*. London: Routledge.

Reynolds, D., Hopkins, D., Potter, D. and Chapman, C. (2001) *School Improvement for Schools Facing Challenging Circumstances: A Review of the Literature*. Paper prepared for the Regional Conferences for Schools Facing Challenging Circumstances, May 2001. London: Department for Education and Employment.

Slavin, R. E. (1996) *Education for All*. Lisse: Swets & Zeitlinger.

Teddlie, C. and Reynolds, D. (2000) *The International Handbook of School Effectiveness Research*. London: Falmer Press.

2 The Politics of Improvement: What Hope Now for Working-Class Kids?

Terry Wrigley

CHAPTER OVERVIEW

The important place of political struggle is seldom far away from the surface in Terry Wrigley's work and in this chapter he characteristically adopts a very personal stance towards the question of improvement. Wrigley critically engages with the research on improvement and effectiveness, posing a similar question to the earlier work of Roger Slee and colleagues asking a question of 'Improvement for whom?' (Slee, Weiner and Tomlinson, 1998). Wrigley's chapter poignantly describes the policy implication of the neo-conservative era in the UK, identifying the personal scale of performance targets on students, on teachers working in difficult schools, and on how the identification and intervention in schools in challenging circumstances is often ill conceived and lacking criticality. It is a polemic which is seldom heard in the canon of school improvement and one which contributes substantially to the debate.

From Socrates to Comenius, Ryland and Dewey, the improvement of education has been linked to the struggle for democracy. In freeing knowledge and values from the control of a medieval hierarchy, the Protestant reformation brought universal literacy early to Scotland and Sweden. For the Chartists, and socialists ever since, education was central to political emancipation.

Of course, the ruling class had their own ideas about what sort of learning to permit. During a period of vicious reaction to the French Revolution abroad and Luddite risings at home, the English philanthropist Hannah Moore, founder of Sunday Schools for the poor, set the tone: 'They learn, on weekdays, such coarse works as may fit them for servants. I allow of no writing for the poor. My object is ... to train up the lower classes in habits of industry and piety.' 'Beautiful is the order of society when each, according to his place, pays willing honour to his superiors' (in Simon, 1960: 133).[1] Schooling for the working class throughout Victorian times consisted of basic literacy and numeracy plus discipline; above all, one must not educate people 'beyond their station in life'.

The struggle continued into the twentieth century. Free grammar school places were offered to a small number of working-class children, while the rest stayed on at elementary school till it was time to leave at age 12 (my grandmother) or 14 (my mother's generation). The frustration and bitterness remain. Each time I visit, my mother says how proud she is of my education. She passed the first stage of the scholarship exam for a grammar school place; her headmistress told her it was pointless her sitting the final part since her family could not possibly afford the uniform. We should remember our history whenever working-class parents are stigmatized as 'culturally deprived'. It has been a long and active process of deprivation.

The comprehensive school system – systematically eroded by New Labour – was probably the biggest school improvement of all. This, and then a common exam system, more than doubled the proportion gaining five A*–C grade GCSEs (formerly GCE O-levels). Comprehensive schools are now standard in all the countries with high scores in the PISA study.[2] Germany's miserable results, on the other hand, sent a shock-wave through its divided system.[3] Of course, comprehensive schools alone do not remove all the causes of underachievement, but they establish a platform on which to build.

The origins of the School Effectiveness paradigm

By the late 1960s, sociologists had clearly established the correlation between parental income/occupation/status and school achievement. Some interesting, though flawed, attempts were made to find theoretical clarifications (e.g., Basil Bernstein's 'language deficit' theory (1971)), and bold but short-lived experiments in curriculum reform (e.g., Eric Midwinter's community school curriculum in Liverpool). In the USA, the Coleman report (1966) clearly demonstrated the link between racial inequality (intertwined with poverty) and school results – a radical challenge to the America of its day. The School Effectiveness paradigm typically writes its own history in terms of a rejection of these links; seeing them as fatalistic, it proclaims itself to be the replacement for such an 'outdated' educational sociology, claiming itself to be more radical because it is more optimistic.[4] Ironically, its own data has repeatedly shown the sociologists' assertions to be correct,[5] but it prefers to push this fact into the background, choosing to foreground the much smaller differences *between* schools serving similar areas – the 'school effect'. (For a more extended critique of the School Effectiveness paradigm and its impact on School Improvement, see Wrigley, 2003: 11–26.) This is not, of course, to suggest that the difference schools make is unimportant, but rather to signal the ideological shift which accompanied this new paradigm in educational research and the advent of the new policy regime.

This shift of focus from social inequalities and towards differential levels of 'school effectiveness' proved immensely attractive to politicians, who in the rightward shift of Neo-Liberalism prefer to relocate the blame for rapidly increasing poverty. With a new emphasis on 'accountability', it was 'failing teachers' and 'failing schools', not the politicians, who were held 'accountable' for growing poverty and despair (see also Mortimore and Whitty, 2000). School Effectiveness research was conveniently used to justify increasing regulation and surveillance of schools through a standardized curriculum, high-stakes testing, performance pay and so on. Though the intensity varied in different states and provinces, this occurred in all the dominant English-speaking countries (USA, UK, Canada, Australia) and has had an influence world-wide thanks to such agencies as OECD and the World Bank.

Of course, these new directions in policy and evaluation also required some positive suggestions – how could schools improve? School Effectiveness sought to identify, by a process of statistical correlation, a list of 'key characteristics' of more 'effective' schools. The methodology was deeply flawed (see Wrigley 2003: 15–18). Among other problems, the vague verbal definitions ('strong leadership', 'a focus on learning') provided little by way of practical guidance, and could be deeply misleading. Their ambiguity enabled politicians to establish a cult of leadership – the 'superheads' who would 'turn round' inner-city schools overnight – and 'effective' teaching geared towards the synchronized transfer of half-digested lumps of knowledge. A new discourse – 'delivering' the curriculum through 'direct' teaching – came into fashion. Teachers became 'competent' technicians, not reflective and caring professionals.[6]

The policy shift was accelerated at every level of the system through a raft of administrative threats and incentives – frequent and often threatening inspections, assessment 'league tables', performance-related pay, the threat of closure or privatization. Despite the efforts of many School Improvement researchers to introduce a softer language to explain the complex lives and development of schools – vision, school culture, ethos, co-operation – the hard rain began to fall. It became extremely difficult to swim against the tide.

The impact on schools serving disadvantaged communities

This new regime affected all schools, but most seriously those in areas of deprivation, whether multiethnic inner-cities or the largely white populations of public housing schemes. (I will begin to use the term 'inner-city schools' as a shorthand to cover all urban areas with high levels of poverty.) Overall, examination results rose steadily, but at the cost of curricular relevance, young people's social development and teacher morale. Indeed, by 2000, almost half the teachers qualifying in England were leaving within two or three years. The regime is clearly unsustainable and only the government appears not to know why.

Though results also went up for schools in disadvantaged areas, the gap between these and the more affluent areas remained large, and on some measures grew larger (Gillborn and Mirza, 2000). Pupils in the poorest areas are working harder, but, in relative terms, when competing for employment, their qualifications may be worth no more than before.

By the year 2000, government statistics provide clear evidence, at age 11, of a substantial overlap between the most successful schools in the poorest areas and the least successful in the most affluent. By age 16, there is virtually no overlap at all. Indeed, the most successful schools in the poorest areas barely reach national average (DfES Autumn Package, published annually; also Ofsted, 2000). Working-class pupils fall further behind the average the longer they are in school. According to David Bell (2003), England's Chief Inspector for Schools, the socio-economic attainment gap has increased in secondary schools:

> Since 1996, the socio-economic attainment gap has narrowed in primary schools but it has widened somewhat in secondary schools. By the age of 16 years, 81 per cent of pupils whose parents are in 'higher professional occupations' gain at least five good GCSE passes, compared with 32 per cent of pupils whose parents have what are defined as 'routine occupations'.

Although, in 2003, there was apparently a sudden improvement in results of schools in the poorest areas, this is largely because of a disruption in the statistics. Schools under severe pressure to improve results – in many cases, under threat of closure and privatization – have realized that an Intermediate GNVQ in Information Technology counts as four good GCSE grades, and that this can be achieved very successfully through a distance-learning package.[7] This is certainly a quick-fix way of improving results, but genuine improvement? It can be done without teacher development, or any serious change in the school. The change in their fortunes may give some schools a boost of confidence and help them commit to real improvement. It will provide a stay of execution for those threatened with closure and provide many pupils with a marketable qualification. The price to be paid is a desperate narrowing of the curriculum, of what counts as a good education, of what counts as achievement. Despite the benefits of less 'academic' qualifications and more situated learning, it is difficult to accept that ICT skills can *substitute* for English, mathematics, Spanish, history and drama.

The proportion of young people entering university is rising towards the 50 per cent mark, but there are big differences across the population. Four out of five university students come from non-manual worker families, but only 2 per cent are the children of unskilled manual workers (Plummer, 2000: 38–9; for further information, see Mittler, 2001: 47–60).

Ostensibly to improve schooling for the poorest families, the Conservative government of the early 1990s determined that schools failing to meet certain standards would be placed in 'special measures' after inspection. The label 'failing schools' soon caught on. Despite a change in government, and many amendments to the inspection framework, this designation remained. Not surprisingly, the majority of such schools are in areas of severe poverty. Without wishing to deny that some schools in disadvantaged neighbourhoods are extremely troubled, it is important to understand how much the system is rigged against schools serving areas of disadvantage, since low examination results steer inspectors forcefully towards negative judgements about teaching and school leadership.

This, and the publication of comparative results in 'league tables', have made it positively dangerous for keen young teachers to work in inner-city schools. Such a choice has always required a sense of vocation and dedication, but now they can find their careers ruined if their test results are below national average, or even by the very fact of having worked at a 'failing' or low-achieving school. On top of the general teacher crisis described earlier, and high housing costs in London, this factor has exacerbated the staffing crisis for inner-city schools.

The accountability regime by which education is controlled in many English-speaking countries and elsewhere has not served well those very pupils who most need better schools. A shift of attention is needed which will re-create schools as communities and provide the opportunities for engagement in learning. In Michael Fullan's words (1999: 19):

> Poor performing students do not need more pressure, they need greater attachment to the school and motivation to want to learn. Pressure by itself in this situation actually demotivates poor performing students.

Government initiatives to help schools in poorer areas

Levels of poverty are extremely high in Britain. In Scotland, almost a third of children are living below the official poverty level, and in inner London it is half. It would be unfair to suggest a lack of official concern about inner-city schools, and there have been some bold initiatives. The problem is they have been undermined by the structural and cultural defects of the broad policy regime. A key example is the Education Action Zones (EAZs), established as local clusters of inner-city schools which would seek new and creative solutions. Firstly, EAZ coordinators and headteachers had to divert their limited energies to securing scarce commercial funding. Second, they were forced into short-term initiatives by the demand that they improve test results within 18 months to two years, undermining more imaginative and far-sighted reforms.

To improve standards of literacy, particularly in poorer areas, new methods of teaching reading were imposed: the 'literacy hour'. Many features of this reform were based on successful innovative practices from Western Australia's 'First Steps' initiative (e.g., collective discussion of texts, a focus on genre), but it also jettisoned well-established home-grown methods (time for individuals to read aloud to a teacher, some opportunity to choose books of personal interest, parental involvement, literacy integrated with other subjects). It was introduced in a way which broke all accepted principles of school improvement theory (winning a consensus, deep understanding, encouraging teachers to be reflective and responsive in adapting practices to local circumstances and the needs of their pupils).[8] The literacy hour in primary schools has had mixed success. It raised test scores at age 11 in its first year, and particularly for boys, though even this is contested.[9] The statistics show no incremental benefit of children following these methods for more than one year. Most dangerous of all, a recent study (Sainsbury, 2003) shows that fewer children now enjoy reading:[10] a damning outcome if we are truly interested in sustainable improvement and lifelong learning. There has been no measurable improvement in standards of writing; in fact, there is no time to write meaningfully within the 15–20 minute slots into which the literacy hour is divided, and because literacy is disconnected from the rest of the curriculum, there are few opportunities for purposeful and engaged writing as opposed to mere exercises.

When the PISA study showed that standards of literacy were quite high in England, a government spokesperson absurdly claimed that this was a result of the literacy hour. (PISA's 15-year-olds had left primary school before the new system was introduced.) Interestingly, PISA data for Scotland showed equally high results, despite higher average levels of poverty, no literacy hour and a refusal to introduce the high-pressure high-surveillance regime of the English system. Sadly, a few Scottish local education authorities have begun to impose similar methods of literacy teaching as a form of 'early intervention', though early results show little positive effect and at least one authority is now emphasizing the importance of play-based learning for children in more deprived communities.

Scotland's greater emphasis on improving 'social capital' is part of a wider policy framework which places an equal emphasis on social values and inclusion as examination results. Scotland has resolutely avoided the English model of creating 57 varieties of schools (with creeping privatization and selection), preferring a more egalitarian model of local comprehensive schools. Its New Community School initiative links various types of social provision to a school or cluster of schools. Given a widespread moral panic about 'young people nowadays', it is remarkable that social development is not a higher priority for school improvement in England and similar countries.

Achievement

Real school improvement requires not only good management techniques but a deep discussion of social and educational purpose. What sort of young people do we want to create? What kind of world do we want to live in? This is the crucial difference between the narrow technical discourse of School Improvement in its hegemonic English-speaking version, and the debates about educational change in many other places. Even in Britain and the USA, we find substantial efforts to change schools for the better which are simply not displayed on the School Improvement shelf.[11]

When reflecting on some exciting developments in schools serving Pakistani and Bangladeshi communities, I wrote the following paragraph:

> Achievement means much more than examination results. We need young people who are skilled tabla players and computer users, who enjoy Asian films and Western books who are able to lead themselves and their communities forward through change and storm and a calm sea, who are socially aware and morally committed and no one's fool. We need a very wide definition of achievement. (Wrigley, 1997)

We speak of vision-building, but how often do we really help teachers engage in dialogue with students and parents to form a definition of desirable achievement? This is not to suggest that examination results are not important. Indeed, if you live in the wrong end of town, or your skin is the wrong colour, you need your certificates more than anybody – but they are never enough. It takes a lot more to see you through.

Ironically, it is not an 'either/or': either examination success or those achievements which are less easy to measure. In truth, schools in poorer areas have to place a high value on all kinds of achievement in order to become rich learning communities.

Beyond managerialism

Genuine improvement requires close attention to five key aspects of the school:

- teaching and learning
- the curriculum
- school ethos
- the wider community
- the leadership and development process.

The dominant model of School Improvement, within a high-surveillance system, recognizes their value, but in a distorted and limiting sense. Particularly in the most deprived areas, an empowerment culture is needed in all five.

In the officially approved version of School Improvement, *teaching* is evaluated according to its efficiency in transmitting precisely the knowledge needed for the next test. The target for 11-year-olds in science involves learning the names of the internal organs of the body, though not what they do – absurdly, that is kept till later! On the other hand, 7-year-olds are judged partly upon the correct use of punctuation, so that's what you teach, whether they are ready for this or still struggling with more funda-mental aspects of early literacy. The recent emphasis on 'thinking skills' is viewed largely as an add-on, rather than as informing long-term intel-lectual development; 'thinking' doesn't seem to involve critical literacy.

The *curriculum* has been regarded almost as beyond debate. It must be standardized so that all children can be tested on it. Where change is allowed, it is mainly for schools which have already proven their success in the standardized curriculum.[12] There is still no serious thinking about curriculum adaptation for inner city schools, other than an increased vocational relevance – a necessary but insufficient basis.

In the official perspective, *school ethos* is viewed instrumentally, as a means to an end.[13] School as a place where children learn to live and work together, to value diversity, to empathize with each other, to be caring – these are seen as less important than making an orderly space for efficient knowledge transfer.

Likewise, *community links* are viewed one-sidedly as a way to improve results. The emphasis is on the parent's duty of pushing their children through the school gate in the morning, completed homework in hand; but there is little mutual communication, scant respect for the difficulty and singularity of their lives, and (only in the most successful urban schools) rarely a sense that the school can serve as a focus for community development and social change.

Finally, the study of leadership and school development processes has become divorced from the other four aspects. Fred Inglis put his finger on the problem:

> Managerialism conceals the will to power by appeals to the fulfilment of purely technical imperatives ... Managerialism only retains its power by suppressing moral-political argument ... Technicism offers itself as value-free. (Inglis, 1989: 42–5)

He called for a 'remoralization' of the way schools are run. We seriously limit our understanding if we deconteztualize and depoliticize the process. Improving schools in areas of deprivation involves a serious engagement with the local community, its experiences, its aspirations. 'Turning a school round' is a wiser metaphor than most people understand: it is not just a matter of raising results, it requires turning the school round to face its community and to provide for some of its pressing needs.

A managerial approach to school development produces more of the same, faster but not necessarily better. It produces shallow learning, and often reinforces the very patterns and processes which inadvertently discriminate and disengage. It mistakes intensification for improvement.

A community curriculum

The curriculum is not a parcel to be 'delivered', but a space to find and make meaning. School improvers cannot just take it for granted. Re-designing the curriculum for changing times should be central to our project. This is not just a question of modernization, but a deeply political issue, given the unprecedented global concentration of wealth and power. Helping young people to understand the big issues of environment, development and war could be a matter of life and death for many.

England's National Curriculum of the 1990s was technologically advanced but socially reactionary. As well as promoting scientific and technological understanding, a curriculum for the twenty-first century will need to

- challenge the injustice of racism and poverty;
- promote concerned understanding and active citizenship;
- develop critical literacy across a range of media;
- remove pressure from young children, and re-establish learning through play;
- raise the status of the creative and performing arts, social development and health.

All these are important for the most deprived communities, but we should also focus on their particular needs. Despite the standardized curriculum, we have held onto some concept of 'multicultural curriculum' but do not have a word for adapting a curriculum for white working-class children – a 'community curriculum' perhaps? Vocational experiences are important but only part of the answer. More situated learning can also be related to social needs – whether designing a playground (design and technology), measuring the insulation in your rented flat (science), or making a video in a campaign for a new zebra crossing (English). Nineteenth-century socialists campaigning against utilitarianism (the vocationalism of its day) demanded for their children '*really* useful knowledge ... concerning our conditions in life ... and how to get out of our present troubles' (Johnson, 1979).

Of course 'basic skills' are important, but they are broader than normally construed. Literacy is central, but must extend to critical literacy and media education. Those who struggle most in learning to read and write are not helped by the diet of decontextualized exercises which is often fed to the 'remedial class'.

A respect for their families, their lives, their daily struggle to survive and bring up the children, their neighbourhoods – however damaged – and a constructive hope for the future, are as important in the public housing schemes as in the multicultural communities of the inner city. All children need to respect diverse cultures; minority pupils need to have their cultural heritage respected, while gaining access to the cultural capital of the majority.

When studying some schools with many bilingual pupils, I discovered an unusual pedagogy which, for want of a more elegant expression, I can only call 'cultural reflection and repositioning' (Giroux might call it 'border pedagogies'). Often using the arts as a medium, it involved an open-ended exploration of cultural heritage, but with the space for pupils to rethink and reposition themselves if they wished. For example,

Muslim pupils wrote their own creeds, which normally began with orthodox quotations from the Quran, but quickly moved to expressing their deeply felt values in a present-day context. Such a pedagogy would be valuable for all young people, whether questioning racism, sexism, or the all-pervasive consumerism.[14]

School is a house of learning

There is now frequent discussion in the School Improvement literature of 'learning communities'. We need to extend and connect this in two directions: to a discussion of schools as 'living communities' – places where young people can enjoy being together and developing into adults – and 'communities of concern' – where learning embodies empathy and caring as well as intellectual scrutiny.

Given the widespread demonization of young people, particularly those in areas of poverty, as well as a more balanced concern that children now have less secure family lives than previous generations, school improvement strategies ought to pay more attention to schools as communities. This goes beyond an instrumental emphasis on school ethos (as a means to the end of raising attainment) to a deep concern for the lives of young people – the ten or twelve years of their lives they spend in school – and school as the place where they learn to be adult members of the society.

In the mid-1990s, a German conference entitled 'School is a House of Learning' (Bildungskommission NRW, 1995) drew up the following mission statement:

- a place where everybody is welcome, where learners and teachers are accepted in their individuality;
- a place where people are allowed time to grow up, to take care of one another and be treated with respect;
- a place whose rooms invite you to stay, offer you the chance to learn, and stimulate you to learn and show initiative;
- a place where diversions and mistakes are allowed, but where evaluation in the form of feedback gives you a sense of direction;
- a place for intensive work, and where it feels good to learn;
- a place where learning is infectious.

This quality of living is a prerequisite in working-class areas for improving learning. The school environment and its relationships mediate and symbolize the respect which should be given to these young people, in contrast to the disrespect they and their families experience as a result of poor housing, low pay and bad headlines.

It is very different from what often passes as an 'ethos of achievement', involving increasing pressure to perform – and the feeling of inadequacy when, constantly measured, they just cannot measure up.

One of the negative consequences of creating new comprehensive schools by merging former grammar schools and secondary modern schools has been an increase in school size. There were many reasons for this: decisions based on a wide choice of options for older pupils; the decision to divide pupils of a particular age into many levels based on their different 'abilities'.

The consequence: 11 to 14-year-olds in British secondary schools face 12 to 15 different teachers each week. This makes many recent recommendations for improving learning almost impossible – more attention to individual differences, to preferred learning styles, to special educational needs and so on. It is particularly damaging to young people who have less social capital, weaker parental support, greater learning difficulties, or chaotic home lives.

This is in sharp contrast with the pattern in Scandinavian schools. In Norway for example, 11 to 16-year-olds are generally taught by no more than five different teachers, each covering two or three subjects. These form year teams, not subject departments – a small group of teachers who share responsibility for the teaching, personal guidance and learning support of 100 or so young people of a particular age. They know their pupils well, keep in close contact with their families, and monitor their intellectual and social development.

Similar patterns are increasingly being adopted elsewhere. The Coalition of Essential Schools, in the USA, believes that no teacher should have responsibility for teaching more than 80 or 90 children, a maximum of four or five different classes. The Coalition regards this as important not only for the emotional and social development of young people, but also as a means to promote learning in depth, rather than a rush to cover every detail in the curriculum.[15]

In recent School Improvement texts, there is a greater emphasis on culture than structure, but we should understand the relationship between the two: structure often constrains culture, providing the circumstances and boundaries within which cultural change is possible. Real improvement of schools for young people growing up in troubled environments may depend precisely upon such a structural transformation.

The concept of 'communities of concern' was once articulated by Noam Chomsky in a critique of learning as the accumulation of facts.

> They [the students] should not be seen merely as an audience but as a part
> of a community of common concern in which one hopes to participate
> constructively. We should be speaking not to but with ... Students don't
> learn by a mere transfer of knowledge, consumed through rote memori-
> zation and later regurgitated. True learning comes about through the
> discovery of truth, not through the imposition of an official truth. That
> never leads to the development of independent and critical thought. It is
> the obligation of any teacher to help students discover the truth and not to
> suppress information and insights that may be embarrassing to the wealthy
> and powerful people who create, design, and make policies about schools.
> (Chomsky, 2000: 21)

There is an important consideration for all today's young people: what
is the combined impact of the rapidly changing images which fly past
their consciousness through television, and the drizzle of facts from their
teachers' instruction in school? For young people whose lives are full of
many more pressing problems, the establishment of the classroom and
school as a *community of concern* is a key aspect of building a 'learning
community'.

The re-creation of schools and classrooms as communities of concern
involves deep changes in learning. One of New York's 'essential schools'
tackled this by establishing a common code of practice, 'The Promise',
for learning across the curriculum. This metacurriculum helps to engage
young people as active, critical, concerned learners. The Promise sets
expectations for students and teachers to deepen learning in whatever
they pursue. In each project, students are guided by five core questions:

- *Viewpoint*: From whose viewpoint are we hearing this? To whom
  are they speaking? Would this look different if she or he were in
  another place or time?
- *Evidence*: How do we know what we know? What evidence will
  we accept? How credible will such evidence appear to others? What
  rules of evidence are appropriate to different tasks?
- *Connections and patterns*: How are things connected together?
  Have we ever encountered this before? Is there a discernible pattern
  here? What came first? Is there a clear cause and effect? What are
  the probable consequences that might follow from taking course x
  rather than course y? How probable? Is this a 'law' of causality, a
  probability, or a mere correlation?
- *Conjecture*: What if things had been different? Suppose King
  George had been a very different personality? Suppose Napoleon or
  Martin Luther King Jr or Hitler had not been born? Suppose King's

assassin had missed? (Our fourth habit encompassed our belief that a well educated person saw alternatives, other possibilities, and assumed that choices mattered. They could make a difference. The future was not, perhaps, inevitable.)

- And finally – who, after all, cares? Does it *matter*? And to whom? Is it of mere 'academic' interest, or might it lead to significant *changes* in the way we see the world and the world sees us? (Meier, 1998: 607–8).

Culture

One of the most important contributions of School Improvement theory has been a shift of emphasis from lists of 'key characteristics of effective schools' to a more holistic examination of 'school culture'. In my experience, as a visitor to many schools, the 'key characteristics' only make a difference provided the culture is healthy. For example, in a negative climate, an increased use of assessment can be counterproductive, because of the damaging way in which data is collected and used.

These are early days, and the accounts of culture we read in School Improvement research are often rather threadbare compared with the 'thick description' of which anthropologists and other ethnographers are proud (Geertz, 1973). School visits are sometimes too hurried to really appreciate the meanings which participants derive from objects, behaviours or rituals. The consequence is often that the researcher falls back on traditional categories to explain these schools, or relies uncritically on the widespread and officially approved discourse of managerialist accountability and surveillance.

I have written of the need for an empowerment culture in all the major aspects of school life: pedagogy, curriculum, ethos, community links and the school development process itself (see Wrigley, 2000). This is in contrast with the prevailing 'surveillance culture' of the English education system, for example, and contrary to the insistence in some School Effectiveness texts, and in official advice,[16] that inner-city schools need stricter discipline and a back-to-basics curriculum.

From 'thick descriptions' of case study schools, we need to develop a theorized account of why some school cultures have a positive impact on the learning of young people. Cultural leadership for school improvement requires a more political and contextualized exploration of culture than we have managed so far, and specifically in relation to demands for greater democracy and to the achievement of success in inner-city schools. For example:

- exploring the differences between authoritarian and cooperative cultures, including developing new rituals for cooperative and democratic learning;
- examining the cultural significance of alienated forms of learning, in which, like factory work, you are told what to write and then hand over your product not to an interested audience but to the teacher-as-examiner, for token payment in the form of a mark or grade;
- questioning the culture of target setting and surveillance which regulates the lives of pupils and teachers, and exploring more democratic forms of educational responsibility than the present accountability culture;
- examining the cultural messages of classrooms which are dominated by the teacher's voice, closed questions and rituals of transmission of superior wisdom;
- developing a better understanding of cultural difference, in order to prevent high levels of exclusion;
- understanding how tacit assumptions about 'ability' and 'intelligence' are worked out symbolically in classroom interactions;
- discovering how tacit assumptions about single parents and 'dysfunctional' working class families operate symbolically in classroom interactions (Wrigley, 2003: 36–7).

Social justice

There is scant attention to social inequalities and power differences in the mainstream School Improvement literature of English-speaking countries. Issues of race and social class which are so important in understanding schools in difficulty are absent or only marginally included. This is not because little is known about such questions, but because these concerns and ideas are regarded as beyond the territory of School Improvement. In its early days, perhaps the emerging School Improvement paradigm had to concentrate on finding some generic features of leadership and change management. It is increasingly clear that a generic understanding which does not engage theoretically with issues of equality and social justice is not assisting inner-city schools.

In the absence of a theoretical understanding, discussion of inequality can result in a deficit discourse. This applies across a wide range of questions, from behavioural problems (the scientifically dubious 'ADHD' label), the boys' underachievement issue, language deficit arguments, asylum seekers and so on (see Wrigley, 2003: 153–83). This occurs within a political climate where real individuals and communities figure as obstacles to reaching numerical targets, rather than as people with real qualities and needs. The dissemination of myths about working-class communities – uniformly dysfunctional, 'concrete jungles', inner cities as wild and dangerous territory full of 'illegals' – take the place of reasoned and balanced sociological exploration.

We need a much closer understanding of the lives and learning of working-class families. I remember the influences on my own learning, growing up in a street of Victorian terraced houses without bathrooms, just outside toilets. (Not an easy place to have a quiet read away from the TV!) Nobody in our street had been to university, but I learnt to play chess from an old man on his doorstep. I acquired a fascination for foreign languages when a Swiss mental health nurse moved in next door. I collected (almost literally) a store of geographical knowledge from the corner grocer who supplied me with tea varieties and maps of India for my school project. I was introduced to Shakespeare, the King James Bible, and Handel's *Messiah* by Aunty Doris, a self-educated intellectual who had left school at 14 and who, by good fortune and kind support, had nevertheless qualified as a district nurse. I was 21, on a PGCE course, when I learnt that people like myself were 'culturally deprived'. Teachers know little about the cultural fabric of the inner city, and less still about the skills, knowledge and personal qualities which may reside in some corners of public housing schemes, and which are certainly in evidence in the multiculture of the inner city.[17] There has been much more social segregation in the years since I grew up, and perhaps a greater concentration of poverty, unemployment and disturbance in many housing schemes than in the working-class communities of the 1950s and 1960s. Nevertheless, it is time that we balanced a positive understanding against the denigration and low expectations, and that we develop more community schools which promote and draw upon the talent of the local community.

The way forward

The study of school development and educational change has a challenging future. Great strides have been made in the last decade in understanding the processes of school change and leadership, particularly in parts of Britain, America, Canada and Australia in this period.

Because of our pride in this achievement, it is difficult to realize that the twin paradigms of School Effectiveness and School Improvement, as they have established themselves in the dominant English-speaking countries, are not universal and certainly not the only ways of conceptualizing improvement and change.[18] Latin American studies of school effectiveness focus far more strongly on poverty and social justice. The German-speaking countries ground their discussion of the change process in a philosophical discussion about the aims of education, and develop specific theory and case study research relating to environmental concerns, gender, social change and so on. There is a wealth of diverse material from urban areas of the United States on educational and social development which we often overlook because it is not generally referenced in canon of Effectiveness and Improvement texts. In Britain, there is a wealth of recent literature classified as sociology or multicultural education or inclusion which could illuminate our work with schools in difficulties, complementing – and sometimes contradicting – the messages of the dominant School Improvement culture.[19]

Those who wish to diminish the attainment gap need to provide a vision of education which moves beyond learning for targets and tests. We need to connect up with this wider educational and social knowledge and develop a more liberating and emancipatory understanding of learning and school culture.

Notes

1 Brian Simon's books provide compelling and extensive evidence of the class basis on which education was established in Britain, as well as the political struggle to improve it.

2 At least up to the age of 15, the age tested under PISA 2000, the international tests covering attainment in language, mathematics and science.

3 A detailed analysis is available in German, *Deutsches PISA-Konsortium* (2001). A summary can be found in English in Baumert and Schümer (2002).

4 D. Reynolds and C. Teddlie, principal gatekeepers of the School Effectiveness paradigm, argue this vision forcefully in a debate with their critics in *School Effectiveness and School Improvement* (2001). For example: 'Thirty years ago there was a widespread belief that 'schools make no difference' which reflected the results of American research (e.g. Coleman *et al.*, 1966 (p. 103); 'School effectiveness is the discipline in which radicals should situate themselves' (p. 111).

5 Reynolds and Teddlie acknowledge this point paradoxically: 'SE researchers are optimistic with regard to the fact that schools can account for 12–15 per cent of the variance in student achievement. Their conclusion would be that the glass is not 85 per cent empty but

rather 15 per cent full, and that 15 per cent can have powerful effects long term' (2001: 54).

6 For critiques of this, see, for example, Mahony and Hextall (2000), and various contributions to Fielding (2001).

7 The DfES *Autumn Package* shows that in 2003, after years of stagnation, the median for schools with over half their pupils entitled to free meals suddenly moved up by 8 percentage points. The output figures used are based on the proportion of 16-year-olds obtaining five or more A*–C grades in the GCSE – 'or the equivalent'. Surprisingly, a pre-vocational GNVQ (General National Vocational Qualification) in Information Technology at intermediate level counts as equivalent to four of these grades. One enterprising school has produced an online distance-learning package for this; its publicity claims that over half of the 50 fastest improving schools in England are using it (www.ttsonline.net/general/projects/ttscourses.html). Some schools have been able to increase the percentage of pupils gaining 'the equivalent of' five A*–C grades dramatically. Going one step further, the Specialist Schools Trust (www.schoolsnetwork.org.uk) is suggesting that the fifth subject can be obtained by entering pupils for a GCSE in computer graphics, with little extra effort because of the substantial overlap with the GNVQ in ICT.

8 Schools were told that they could not be forced to implement it, but they would be 'interrogated' [*sic!*] if they did not (Hunt, 2001). New Labour's command approach to school improvement is further illustrated by an official presentation from the Head of the Standards and Effectiveness unit to the Educational Action Zones conference: 'Beliefs do not necessarily shape behaviour. More usually it's the other way round – behaviours shape beliefs. Only when people have experienced a change do they revise their beliefs accordingly ... Sometimes it is necessary to mandate the change, implement it well, consciously challenge the prevailing culture, and then have the courage to sustain it until beliefs shift' (cited in Jones, 2001).

9 The test questions became easier. They required more factual and less inferential reading. The text used was a factual account of spiders, replacing, in the previous year, an author's fictional and autobiographical reflections on childhood. The national criteria were altered (see Hilton, 2001).

10 The percentage of 11-year-old boys who say they enjoy reading stories dropped from 70 in 1998 to 55 in 2003, a reduction of 15 percentage points, and with girls, from 85 to 75, or 10 percentage points. There was also a decline in enjoyment of reading poems and

information books, of going to the library, and of those who prefer television to reading (Sainsbury, 2003).

11 Until recently, School Improvement literature has tended to ignore teaching and learning, except at a superficial or managerial level. (A key exception in England was David Hopkins (Joyce, *et al.*, 1997, 1999). The gap is even larger in terms of the curriculum studies literature, or special education and inclusion, or 'race' and bilingual pupils, which are hardly ever cited in leadership or improvement texts. See Wrigley (2003: chapters 5–10) for an attempt to re-integrate this wider literature into a broader understanding of School Improvement.

12 'There is no need to remove the national curriculum requirements from successful schools because they are succeeding. Why change things? We have a success. The place where greater freedom is most needed is in those schools which are not succeeding. I tend to believe that the proposal is perverse' (Lord Dearing, May 2002).

13 See, for example, Fielding (1999: 280) or Clarke (2001).

14 The descriptions are to be found in Wrigley (2000). A more theoretical analysis appears in Wrigley (2000a).

15 There is a more extended discussion, drawing on Sergiovanni, in Wrigley (2003: 140, 152).

16 See, for example, the advice that was given by Ofsted on how to 'turn round' a school in special measures.

17 On a personal note, a friend's son became such an expert musician that, at the age of 16, he was flown from England to Toronto to accompany on the tabla a famous professional Indian musician. The headteacher of the secondary school he had attended for five years knew nothing of his talents. How often do such things happen? How many gifts and talents, large or small, go unnoticed in the present drive for exam results?

18 See for example the RINACE website for Latin America www.rinace. org; H. Altrichter *et al.*, (1998) Handbuch zur Schulentwicklung, for the German-speaking countries, or the *Journal der Schulentwicklung*; the journal *Bedre Skole* for Norway; some North American chapters in Hargreaves *et al.* (1998) International handbook of educational change.

19 This is not a critique of academic texts *per se*, but of the ways they connect with the wider policy regime and practices.

References

Altrichter, H., Schley, W. and Schratz, M. (1998) *Handbuch zur Schulentwicklung*. (Handbook for School Development) Innsbruck: StudienVerlag.

Baumert, J. and Schümer, G. (2002) 'Family background, selection and achievement: the German experience' (trans. T. Wrigley), *Improving Schools*, 5, 3.

Bell, D. (2003) 'Access and achievement in urban education: ten years on'. Press release of speech to Fabian Society (20 November). www.ofsted.gov.uk

Bernstein, B. (1971) *Class, Codes and Control, Vol. 1. Theoretical Studies Towards a Sociology of Language*. London: Routledge and Kegan Paul.

Bildungskommission NRW (1995) *Zukunft der Bildung – Schule der Zukunft* (Future of Education – School of the Future) Denkschrift der Kommission 'Zukunft der Bildung – Schule der Zukunft' beim Ministerpräsidenten des Landes Nordrhein-Westfalen. Neuwied.

Chomsky, N. (2000) *Chomsky on Miseducation*. Lanham, MD: Rowman and Littlefield.

Clarke, P. (2001) 'Feeling compromised – the impact on teachers of the performance culture', *Improving Schools*, 4, 3.

Coleman, J.S. *et al.* (1966) *Equality of Educational Opportunity*. Washington, DC: Government Printing Office.

DfES 'Autumn Package' (published annually, archives on website) www.standards.dfes.gov.uk/performance/ap/index.html

Deutsches PISA-Konsortium (eds) (2001) *PISA 2000: Basiskompetenzen von Schülerinnen und Schülern im internationalen Vergleich* (International Comparisons of Pupils' Basic Competences). Opladen: Leske and Budrich.

Fielding, M. (1999) 'Target setting, policy pathology and student perspectives: learning to labour in new times', *Cambridge Journal of Education*, 29, 2.

Fielding, M. (ed.) (2001) *Taking Education Really Seriously: Four Years Hard Labour*. London: RoutledgeFalmer.

Fullan, M. (1999) *Change Forces – The Sequel*. London: Falmer.

Geertz, C. (1973) *The Interpretation of Cultures*. New York: Basic Books.

Gillborn, D. and Mirza, H. (2000) *Educational Inequality: Mapping Race, Class and Gender*. www.ofsted.gov.uk

Hargreaves, A. *et al.* (eds) (1998) *International Handbook of Educational Change*. Dordrecht: Kluwer.

Hilton, M. (2001) 'Are the key stage 2 reading tests becoming easier each year?', *Reading*, 35, 1.

Hunt, G. (2001) 'Democracy or a command curriculum: teaching literacy in England', *Improving Schools*, 4, 3.

Inglis, F. (1989) 'Managerialism and morality: the corporate and the republican school', in W. Carr (ed.) *Quality in Teaching*. London: Falmer.

Johnson, R. (1979) 'Really useful knowledge', in J. Clarke *et al.* (eds) *Working-class Culture: Studies in History and Theory*. London: Hutchinson.

Jones, K. (2001) 'Conclusion: responding to the themes of the collection', in C. Chitty and B. Simon (eds) *Promoting Comprehensive Education in the 21st Century*. Stoke: Trentham.

Joyce, B., Calhoun, E. and Hopkins, D. (1997) *Models of Learning – Tools for Teaching*. Buckingham: Open University Press.

Joyce, B., Calhoun, E. and Hopkins, D. (1999) *The New Structure of School Improvement: Inquiring Schools and Achieving Students*. Buckingham: Open University Press.

Mahony, P. and Hextall, I. (2000) *Reconstructing Teaching: Standards, Performance and Accountability*. London: RoutledgeFalmer.

Meier, D. (1998) 'Authenticity and educational change', in A. Hargreaves *et al.* (eds) *International Handbook of Educational Change*. Dordrecht: Kluwer.

Mittler, P. (2001) *Working Towards Inclusive Education*. London: Fulton.

Mortimore, P. and Whitty, G. (2000) 'Can school improvement overcome the effects of disadvantage?', in T. Cox (ed.) *Combating Educational Disadvantage*. London: Falmer.

Ofsted (2000) *Improving City Schools*. www.ofsted.gov.uk

Plummer, G. (2000) *Failing Working-class Girls*. Stoke: Trentham.

Reynolds, D. and Teddlie, C.(2001) 'Reflections on the critics', *School Effectiveness and School Improvement*, 12, 1.

Simon, B. (1960) *Studies in the History of Education 1780–1870*. London: Lawrence and Wishart.

Sainsbury, M. (2003) *Children's Attitudes to Reading*. Slough: NFER.

Wrigley, T. (1997) 'Raising achievement for Asian pupils', *Multicultural Teaching*, 16, 1.

Wrigley, T. (2000) *The Power to Learn: Stories of Success in the Education of Asian and Other Bilingual Pupils*. Stoke: Trentham.

Wrigley, T. (2000a) 'Pedagogies for improving schools: an invitation to debate', *Improving Schools*, 3, 3.

Wrigley, T. (2003) *Schools of Hope: A New Agenda for School Improvement*. Stoke: Trentham.

3 Learning Disadvantage and Schools in Challenging Circumstances

Richard Riddell

CHAPTER OVERVIEW

Richard Riddell argues cogently for us to take another look at what we are trying to do in our work with schools in challenge. He suggests that the concentration on short-term improvement through targets and goal setting will not bring about a long-term transformation in young people's educational prospects, nor their social and occupational success. In this chapter Ridell draws upon a range of social indicators, with poverty being the most salient, and locates his argument within a frame that he calls learning disadvantage. Cultural capital, as defined through the accumulation, processing, interpretation and sense-making of social encounters, resources and experiences likely to generate real and meaningful connection with the experience of school, is differently defined, he suggests, in the poorer household. As a result, encounters in school are much less likely to make sense for the learner. The assumptions, conventions and organization of the classroom as a learning space are, in Riddell's argument, unlikely to be congruent with life beyond school. In reading this chapter I was reminded of the work of Bernstein (1975) and how the discourse of school improvement has perhaps conveniently, or expediently, avoided the direct connection with matters of social class. In what could become a depressing slide into passive acceptance, Riddell reminds us clearly of the significance and the constant presence of the students' learned experience and I think concludes from a position of optimism and hope. His chapter serves as a reminder that professional educators need to ask the 'why?' questions with their students, school does not have to be as it is – we need to critically engage.

In the evaluation of the knowledge base of children – evaluated when they first arrive in school and during the time they stay in school – the mechanism in general never takes into consideration any 'knowledge from life experience' the children bring with them into school. Thus the poor students are put into a disadvantageous position.

Paulo Freire (1993: 16)

Introduction

I argue here that without policy-makers understanding the learning disadvantage experienced by many young people attending schools in challenging circumstances, the most that can be expected from improvement measures is that many schools are taken off the critical list. Concentration on short-term improvement through attainment targets and better classroom processes, while understandable in a high-stakes external environment, will not bring about a long-term transformation in young people's educational prospects, nor hence their social and occupational success. Furthermore, the gaps in attainment between children of different social classes, so pronounced in England, may narrow but are likely to remain.

Learning disadvantage arises when young people's circumstances impair their functioning as learners or prevent their previous learning from being accessed in the classroom. It derives from social and material disadvantage but also arises when the dominant culture and expectations of school are at odds with those of family or community.

In major English cities, where many schools facing challenging circumstances are located, the school system has undergone a profound process of stratification over the past 30 years. In many secondary schools – sometimes the majority in some areas – learning disadvantage now predominates and there are comparatively few students likely to attain national benchmarks at the age of 16. Countering learning disadvantage is these schools' principal educational task.

Understanding learning disadvantage

Socially based differences in educational outcome are stark in the UK. Only 30 per cent of the children of unskilled manual parents achieve five GCSE A*–C grades compared to 59 per cent of children of managerial or professional parents. In housing terms, only 19 per cent of children whose parents live in council-rented property achieve five A*–C grades, whereas 57 per cent do so of children of parents who own their own homes. There are differences even by the age of five when performance in cognitive development tests of children in deprived areas lags an average 3.7 per cent behind that of children from homes with incomes in the top fifth (*ibid.*).

These differences in performance are complemented by physical differences. Children in Social Class V are less likely than their peers in Social Classes I and II to achieve recommended nutrient levels and are more likely by age 15 to report longstanding illness (Howard *et al.*, 2001;

Bradshaw, 2002). They are also smaller, the difference being 2.25 centi-
metres by age five, following the greater likelihood of low birthweight
(Howard *et al.*, 2001).

The physical basis for differing educational performance is perhaps
the easiest to understand. The 32 per cent of children living in poverty
in England, who may come to school hungry, feeling unwell or possibly
upset by the emotional turmoil in their lives, will not approach learning
with the enthusiasm and confidence evinced by many of their more
socially advantaged peers (Whitty, 2002). With 'the highest child poverty
rate in the European Union' (Bradshaw, 2002: 17), this group of children
is particularly important in England. However, it does not encompass by
any means all those who may experience learning disadvantage.

The much broader circumstances in which such disadvantage may
arise can be appreciated from consideration of the model of the learning
process shown in Figure 3.1, developed from an ethnographic study of
the relation between factors in children's backgrounds and their lives in
school (Pollard with Filer, 1996). The influences on what children bring
to their learning in the classroom are represented in the model and the
potentially cumulative nature of disadvantage (or advantage), because of
learning's cyclical nature, becomes obvious.

Children enter classrooms (referred to in Figure 3.1 as 'opportunity to
learn in social settings') with the levels of self-confidence and motivation
as learners, and the 'strategic resources' (skills and approaches to
learning), they have developed from previous experience, in school and
out. These are rooted in the material, cultural and linguistic resources, as
Figure 3.1 expresses it, invested in them up to this point.

Examples of material resources include the nature and quality of the
children's homes, the books and toys they have outside school and various
non-school experiences such as going to the theatre or visiting places
of interest. Cultural resources include their accumulating knowledge of
how to interpret, behave and gain acceptance in differing social contexts,
including school. Linguistic resources include their development in home
or other languages, their ability to use language to support their learning
and their understanding and capacity to react appropriately within the
predominant language patterns they encounter, including in the classroom.
Do they recognize the expectations held by adults of children, for example,
as reflected in the common forms of questioning or address? Are they able
to react and communicate in ways which are recognized and rewarded and
avoid being judged to be inadequate (National Research Council, 2000)?

Because of learning's cyclical nature, previous successful learning and
greater resources will have enhanced the self-confidence, motivation and

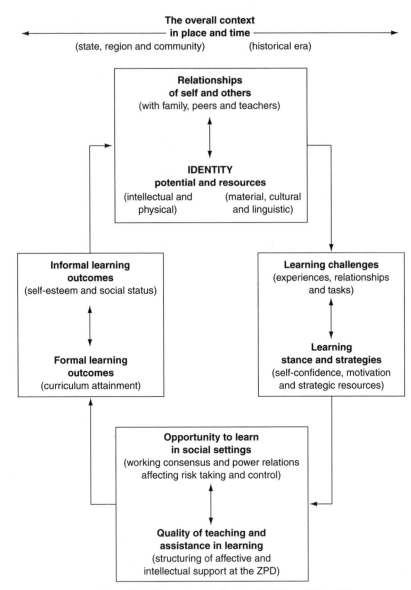

Figure 3.1: A social model of learning (Pollard with Filer, 1996: 97)

strategic resources which make further learning success likely. Success is likely to be followed by further success; comparative failure is likely to be followed by more of the same. It is easy to understand on this basis how the increasing attainment gaps by age 16, commented on by Gillborn and Mirza (2000), have arisen.

While schools enable young people to accumulate material, cultural and linguistic resources as the result of their experiences at school, the importance of young people's experiences for the 53 per cent of their time (excluding sleep) they spend in their home and community (National Research Council, 2000) cannot be underestimated. If children's lives are impoverished socially and materially outside school and go on being so throughout their school careers, it is difficult to develop a mutually reinforcing relationship between learning in all aspects of their lives. It is more difficult for the experiences provided at home to complement and reinforce what is being studied at school.

But even if family and community life is not impoverished, if the expectations of home differ from, conflict with, or do not relate to, those of school, the cultural and material resources young people bring to the classroom will be impaired. The learning of these young people, often from white working-class backgrounds, will be disadvantaged cumulatively. Their disadvantage may be exacerbated if they use linguistic patterns differing from those of school and which engender limiting assumptions among the staff about their potential. Even assuming motivation, the young people may not be clear about the nature of educational success expected by school and the implications for the way they should work and conduct themselves.

Other young people, such as those from some minority communities, may have rich cultural and other experiences outside school but may not be able to draw on them fully in the classroom. This may be because the learning they have accumulated elsewhere – wrapped up in particular circumstances, groupings, emotions and linguistic and other norms – may not *transfer* to the different circumstances of the classroom (Claxton, 1999; National Research Council, 2000), unless sympathetic attempts are made to build effective bridges. These young people, who may be very effective learners in other contexts, may also be disadvantaged and unable to call on all their resources which could potentially be useful. The difficulty of ineffective transfer may be compounded further for those young people who move regularly between several different cultural and social contexts – for example, if they come from communities of Asian origin (Wrigley, 2000) – and their experience and learning may become compartmentalized.

Although poverty has severe effects on learning, therefore, a much broader group of young people may suffer from learning disadvantage because the assumptions, conventions and organization of the classroom, and the basis of the learning experiences provided there, can be so different and *distant* from the other contexts in their lives in which they learn.

Learning disadvantage in urban areas

Most state secondary schools in England will have some children suffering learning disadvantage; many schools will have many. But in urban areas the majority of young people may be affected in certain schools. Economic and social change has brought about much greater concentrations of children suffering from social and material disadvantage. The average level of free school meals, for example, in the 620 secondary schools first identified for support from the Schools Facing Challenging Circumstances scheme was 36 per cent against a national average of nearly 20 per cent (Hopkins *et al.*, 2001). But the highest figure was 84 per cent.[1]

At the same time, the quasi-market introduced into the education service in a number of English-speaking countries (Whitty *et al.*, 1998) has enabled the flight of middle-class parents from certain urban schools, narrowing the social nature of their intake (Riddell, 2003). This has increased the proportion of young people in urban schools likely to experience learning disadvantage in the broader forms described.

Middle-class parents, playing the admissions and appeals system effectively, have exercised their preference in favour of schools attended by 'people like us' in urban areas and against schools with substantial numbers of working-class pupils or from ethnic minorities (Ball *et al.*, 1995; Bagley *et al.*, 2001; Ball, 2003). Urban areas have never really benefited anyway from the comprehensive schools developed in rural areas and market towns which continue to be patronized by parents from all social backgrounds (Brighouse, 2002). And in London, the development of comprehensive policies was accompanied by the move of voluntary-aided grammar schools into the private sector, without significant change in the social nature of their intakes (Newsam, 1998). As in other UK cities, they joined an already thriving sector whose social catchment was to remain narrow, despite the Assisted Places Scheme (Edwards and Whitty, 1997). In some areas in England, including cities, grammar schools were also retained.

The secondary school system in major cities has become highly stratified as a consequence. Besides the disproportionate effects on the state system of the private sector, there are now schools in the higher strata of the state system which are 'super-selective', because they are grammar or specialist schools, or their intake has become socially advantaged (Newsam, 2002) through the quasi-market or 'selection by mortgage'. There may be some 'median comprehensive schools', as Brighouse (2002) terms them, with a broad social intake and a fair spread of young people likely to achieve five A*–C grades at GCSE, but these schools are likely to be a minority. On the other hand, there will be many schools such as those Brighouse refers to as 'comprehensive minus' or 'secondary modern minus', where the social nature of the intake is narrow and the likely outcomes at 16 do not approach national benchmarks.

These 'bottom strata schools' (Riddell, 2003) predominate in many city communities. Because of the loss to these schools over the years of many children of 'aspirant parents' (DfEE, 1999), the consequent narrow social nature of their intake and just the sheer deprivation in the communities they serve, their pupils start behind in their learning and continue to do so. The learning potential of the experiences they continue to have outside school remains poor or inaccessible when they step through the classroom door. However good the teaching and the classroom processes, it is difficult to make up for this disadvantage; the equivalent 'quality' of teaching in schools in the upper strata will add greater amounts of value.

Countering learning disadvantage

So, bottom strata schools – largely schools in challenging circumstances – will undoubtedly benefit from focusing on learning and teaching, generating positive relationships, providing a clear vision and high expectations, improving the environment, providing time and opportunities for collaboration, distributing leadership and engaging the community as the National College for School Leadership recommends (NCSL, 2002). But unless deeper questions are asked about learning disadvantage – why young people continue to be seemingly disadvantaged despite apparently satisfactory processes in classrooms – there will be no fundamental contribution to redressing the educational imbalance. Learning disadvantage is the issue which must be addressed by the first strategy of the NCSL and is the warp to the weft of all eight of NCSLs; it provides the context for generalized school improvement approaches in schools in challenging circumstances; and above all, it is the learning manifestation of often-ignored social changes which make difficult the achievement of the intended outcomes of current national policy (Whitty, 2002).

So what can be done by schools? They cannot eliminate poverty or themselves change the stratified system in which they have to operate. But they can and must build effective bridges between the worlds young people inhabit outside school – the ways of thinking and learning, signs and symbols, and construals of meaning – and the learning experiences they plan for them inside. Even though schools' purpose, or one of them at least, is to induct young people irrespective of background into recognized formal knowledge domains and structures (the 'canon'), teaching must be scaffolded round the mental worlds of their pupils as they continuously develop in peer group, family and community. Otherwise, the otherness or artificiality of the world of school and abstract knowledge become increasingly emphasized and, with age, are seen to be more and more arcane and irrelevant, progressively inhibiting learning.

Schools need to draw on the *funds of knowledge* which exist in all communities, even the most impoverished (Moll and Greenberg, 1992). These are the means through which young people develop their identities and find meaning. They underpin work, communication, social life, relationships, bringing up children, keeping up a home and so on. Funds of knowledge are built from experience and inherited through family and community history – for example, from life in another UK city or Kosovo. They include the what of knowledge (the things which are actually known in a community), the how (the ways in which learning is accumulated) and the social and cultural contexts in which learning occurs. These contexts outside school, in which young people spend most of their time as they grow up, provide familiar surroundings for them and, when encountered, predispose them to further learning, even when they do not recognize it.

For children whose family and community life is already full of the funds of knowledge drawn on extensively in schools – abstract knowledge, high culture, book-based information – and who have social networks replete with people who are successful in the ways recognized and valued by the formal education system, transition to the classroom is easy. They feel comfortable in its social context and expect to learn, knowing what it means; culturally they understand their role and what is expected of them. In terms of Figure 3.1, their high levels of material, cultural and linguistic resources result in a positive stance towards learning and more resources with which to tackle it. These are the benefits often conferred by a middle-class home.

Schools in the bottom strata of the state system need to work at conferring these advantages in relation to school learning themselves, as they are possessed by so few of their pupils. They must seek to understand the predominant funds of knowledge in the community. This cannot be done overnight and requires study and time, but the adults and young people in the community can be tutors for the school and be empowered by the process. Their involvement can be a stepping stone to their fuller engagement in the aims and mission of the school.

Every day, based on this understanding, the school must effect the transition from these other contexts to the learning context of the school,

with its predominant forms of knowledge and quite different arrangements for the association for fixed periods of time of young people with
adults. This involves ensuring the signs and symbols important to young
people in their other contexts become prominent in school, as many
schools have done for years. It means having an expressive order in the
school (Bernstein, 1975) – formal and informal expectations and the
rituals concerning dress and behaviour – focused on the requirements
of learning and its encouragement rather than context-free notions of
authority or appropriate adult/child relations.

Above all, it means making learning activity explicit as soon as the
young people walk through the school door and in all their contacts
with each other and adults. Suitable colour schemes, background music,
furniture and room layouts need to be used. Tools, strategies and
conceptual maps need to be obvious and recognized in displays, classrooms, lessons and all informal gatherings. The school must ensure all
pupils acquire them, as the all-important resources to be brought to
future successful learning cycles, and as the basis for establishing formal
knowledge domains and their navigation as another social and cultural
context for pupils' successful learning. In practice, this means ensuring
the pupils acquire hard and soft thinking skills (Claxton, 1999; National
Research Council, 2000); practise metacognition; develop emotional
literacy (Goleman, 1996) and acquire self-sufficiency in their learning
which can transfer to the rest of their lives.

Success in such a new socio-cultural context for the young people
in these schools means that it must be clearly inhabited by the adults
as well. Although teachers will be doyens of the formal knowledge
domains, the inexact complexity of inducting unique collections of
young minds into them is a matter for developing experience, reflection
and learning, building on the success and failures of others. All adults,
in a learning school which is a professional learning community, need
to be explicit about their own learning and model learning behaviour,
such as the acceptance of mistakes as a natural part of the process. The
model of the relationship between adult and child as pure transmitter of
knowledge onto tabula rasa is not consistent with the nature of learning
itself (National Research Council, 2000) or the provisional nature of
knowledge in the rapidly changing world of the twenty-first century.

Pedagogical support must be provided to enable young people to
make the mental transition back into their community, taking what they
have learnt. There are many strategies which can be used for this such as
studying the community in formal subjects while based in facilities there.
But attempts must also be made to provide some of the relevant and

reinforcing experiences outside school enjoyed by middle-class children, which are another facet of their advantage and a major source of the resources they bring to their learning. This is the importance of out-of-school opportunities for learning, managed wherever possible by parents and the community themselves to avoid the contemporary equivalent of charity for the poor. These opportunities, as a further bridge between the socio-cultural contexts of school and community, should draw on the complementary forms of learning prevalent in more advantaged homes.

The feasibility in the current climate of countering learning disadvantage in schools facing challenging circumstances

None of the work or general approaches advocated here is inconsistent with the paths recommended either by the Handbook for schools facing challenging circumstances (Hopkins *et al.*, 2001) or associated DfES publications and programmes. Drawing on case studies from the IQEA project (Improving the Quality of Education for All), the Handbook advises a three-stage approach to school improvement. The analysis of strengths and weaknesses recommended could include the matters discussed here; the 'learning teams' (actually learning-about-teaching teams) could focus on the identification of learning disadvantage and how, because of cultural assumptions and dominant linguistic patterns in the school's classrooms, the pedagogy was privileging some pupils and not others.

A typical indicative plan submitted for the Leadership Incentive Grant (DfES, 2002b), with its emphasis on the development of extra leadership capacity, could focus this development on learning disadvantage and ways of countering it. And any local education authority plan for schools facing challenging circumstances could similarly include such a focus. The plan's required emphasis on achieving floor targets, possibly by 'sharing good practice' in relation to faculties achieving better results with the same children, would benefit from asking the deeper questions raised here.

Unless these deeper questions of how children learn are asked before decisions are made about how they should be taught, it is likely that the current apparent stubbornness in the data of lower achieving secondary schools will persist. There will – no doubt – be some movement, with the study of best practice in 'data analysis and target-setting' engendering higher aspirations for some young people. Concentration on the children achieving at the borderline of significant benchmarks and development of their strategies for tackling examinations will no doubt lead to some lifting of the attainment scores. This is to be welcomed in the context of a high-stakes (or 'high challenge high support' – DfEE, 2001) scheme like that for schools facing challenging circumstances, where persistent failure to move scores can lead to closure.

What this will not do, however, is transform the learning of young people and harness positively their continuing experiences in peer group, family and community. Without such a change, attainment will most likely reach a new medium-term plateau, similar to that experienced after the introduction of the national literacy and numeracy strategies. Moreover, although 'high challenge high support' may provide a corrective to low expectations, it will also put pressure on schools to look for 'quick wins' and, most important of all, will reduce the capacity and space available for schools to reflect on the why questions in their classrooms rather than just the how. The external accountability mechanisms for a school facing challenging circumstances – not just inspection or the performance tables but the bureaucratic compliance required in relation to the various plans they must complete – will potentially reduce still further their capacity at all levels, certainly for senior management. That the Raising Attainment Plan is supposed to be an integral part of the school improvement plan makes it no less prescriptive or any more integrated. And, challenging circumstances are challenging – the day-to-day circumstances of many of these secondary schools (Riddell, 2003) put pressure on their reflective capacity anyway and their ability to ask the 'why' questions.

Reflective capacity, with the possibility of a return to first principles for the learning of some young people, and the time to do this adequately (making mistakes no doubt as they go), is a corrective required in schools facing challenging circumstances as soon as possible. Although Time for Standards (DfES, 2002a) emphasized professionalism and autonomy as part of the new phase of the reform, and this was echoed in the new national strategy documents for primary and secondary schools (DfES, 2003a, 2003b), it will take some time to change the experience, expectations and ways of working in many schools. The positive professional expectation for change can continue, but the importance to the achievement of national aspirations of schools in the bottom strata of the state system in our major cities needs to be better recognized. The schools need to be party to the creation of positive professional expectation as well as better-organized joint searches for solutions. This could lead to long-term significant change and help address the social class-based gaps in attainment; otherwise, there is a danger that short- or medium-term gains, from huge amounts of effort, will lead to further disillusionment. This would be too high a cost for the young people concerned.

Note

1 The DfES subsequently identified 480 schools qualifying for the scheme on the basis of the 2000 results, reducing to 372 schools in 2001 and 297 in 2002 (DfES website).

References

Bagley, C., Woods, P. and Glatter, R. (2001) 'Rejecting schools: towards a fuller understanding of the process of parental choice', *School Leadership and Management*, 21, 3, 309–25.

Ball, S. (2003) *Class Strategies and the Education Market – The Middle Classes and Social Advantage*. London: RoutledgeFalmer.

Ball, S., Bowe, R. and Gewirtz, S. (1995) 'Circuits of schooling: a sociological exploration of parental choice of school in social-class contexts', *The Sociological Review*, 43, 52–18. Reproduced in Halsey, A. H., Lauder, H., Brown, P. and Stuart Wells, A. (1997) *Education – Culture, Economy and Society*. Oxford: Oxford University Press.

Bernstein, B. (1975) *Class, Codes and Control Volume 3 – Towards a Theory of Educational Transmissions*. London: Routledge and Kegan Paul.

Bradshaw, J. (ed.) (2002) *The Well-being of Children in the UK*. Plymouth: Save the Children.

Brighouse, T. (2002) 'Comprehensive schools then, now and in the future – is it time to draw a line in the sand and create a new ideal?' Text of the Caroline Benn, Brian Simon Memorial Lecture given at the Institute of Education, 28th September.

Claxton, G. (1999) *Wise Up – The Challenge of Lifelong Learning*. London: Bloomsbury.

DfEE (1999) *Excellence in Cities*. London: The Stationery Office.

DfEE (2001) *Schools – Building on Success*. London: The Stationery Office.

DfES (2002a) *Time for Standards – Reforming the School Workforce*. London: DfES.

DfES (2002b) *Leadership Incentive Grant – Guidance*. London: DfES.

DfES (2003a) *A New Specialist System: Transforming Secondary Education*. London: DfES.

DfES (2003b) *Excellence and Enjoyment – A Strategy for Primary Schools*. London: DfES.

Edwards, T. and Whitty, G. (1997) 'Specialisation and selection in secondary education', *Oxford Review of Education*, 23, 1, 5–15.

Freire, P. (1993) *Pedagogy of the City* (trans. Macedo, D.). New York: Continuum.

Gillborn, D. and Mirza, H. (2000) *Educational Inequality – Mapping Race, Class and Gender, A Synthesis of Research Evidence*. London: Ofsted.

Goleman, D. (1996) *Emotional Intelligence – Why it can Matter More than IQ*. London: Bloomsbury.

Hopkins, D., Reynolds, D., Potter, D., Chapman, C. together with Beresford, J., Jackson, P., Sharpe, T., Singleton, C. and Watts, R. (2001) *'Meeting the Challenge' – An Improvement Guide, a Handbook of Guidance and a Review of Research and Practice*. London: DfEE.

Howard, M., Garnham, A., Fimister, G. and Veit-Wilson, J. (2001) *Poverty: The Facts*, 4th edition. London: Child Poverty Action Group.

Moll, L. and Greenberg, J. (1992) *Creating Zones of Possibilities: Combining Social Contexts for Instruction*, in Moll, L. (ed.) *Vygotsky and Education – Instructional Implications and Applications of Sociohistorical Psychology*. Cambridge: Cambridge University Press.

National Research Council (2000) *How People Learn: Brain, Mind, Experience and School*. Washington, DC: National Academy Press.

NCSL (2002) *Making the Difference: Successful Leadership in Challenging Circumstances – A Practical Guide to What Leaders Can Do to Energise Their Schools*. Nottingham: National College for School Leadership.

Newsam, P. (1998) 'How can we know the dancer from the dance?', *Forum*, 40, 1, 4–10.

Newsam, P. (2002) 'Diversity and English secondary schools', unpublished paper for the Secondary Heads' Association.

Pollard, A. with Filer, A. (1996) *The Social World of Children's Learning – Case Studies of Pupils from Four to Seven*. London: Cassell.

Riddell, R. (2003) *Schools for Our Cities – Urban Learning in the Twenty-First Century*. Stoke-on-Trent: Trentham Books.

Whitty, G. (2002) *Making Sense of Education Policy*. London: Paul Chapman.

Whitty, G., Power, S. and Halpin, D. (1998) *Devolution and Choice in Education – The School, the State and the Market*. Buckingham: The Open University Press.

Wrigley, T. (2000) *The Power to Learn – Stories of Success in the Education of Asian and Other Bilingual Pupils*. Stoke-on-Trent: Trentham Books.

4 What is Special about Special Measures? Perspectives from the Inside

Maria Nicolaidou

CHAPTER OVERVIEW

Stories from within school have been the canon of school improvement literature for the past 15 years or so. However, stories from within schools in difficulty have persistently remained an untold tale. In this chapter, the author reports on her work in three schools as a researcher looking into the characteristics of special measures. What we find is a fascinating set of tensions at play, where conflicts of attitude, intervention strategy, role and in particular, power are played out within schools which have to make significant changes evident within very tight timeframes determined by external agencies. The resulting text is challenging and presents the reader with a slight uneasiness – in the words of one headteacher in the chapter 'You're breaking a culture, an educational culture in order to create a new one.'

Introduction

In the past few years, schools in England have been met with unprecedented demands to promote the quality of education that they provide. A national debate was initiated around the nature of school success and effectiveness as the government attempted to 'raise standards'. The initiation of the inspection system delivered through Ofsted since 1993 put forward the notion of 'improving through inspection'. Prior to 1993 the inspection process was made up along the way and there was no precise inspection model or a clear set of criteria against which schools were to be judged. Once the first reports were published, there were many complaints about inconsistencies in judgements (Gray and Hannon, 1996). Thus, the inspections were inconsistent in influence although it was planned otherwise.

Once Ofsted was introduced, the schools received for the first time the inspection handbook that included the criteria against which they would be judged during the inspection. According to Ofsted, therefore, failure is defined in terms of the standards of pupil achievement, the quality of education provided and the efficiency in management and poor provision for pupils' spiritual, moral, social and cultural development. Inevitably, such criteria can only provide a link between teaching and measured outcomes (Winkley, 1999). As a result of the inspection process, areas of strengths and weaknesses are identified. If schools are found not to provide an adequate standard of education, they are either placed in 'special measures' or considered to have 'serious weaknesses'. The outcomes of such an inspection are featured in a report, which is then made public. The public announcement that a school has failed its pupils can be very traumatic for the school, staff, pupils and the broader community. It has been argued that for many in such schools, 'special measures' has had a negative effect on 'morale, resilience, and self-esteem' (Myers and Goldstein, 1998: 177). It is worthwhile to stress here that the post-Ofsted days in a school that has been placed in 'special measures' has been compared to a bereavement period:

> People's reactions to traumatic events such as a death in the family are said to go through a number of stages. Inspection appears to be no different ... the process experienced by most schools and governing bodies ... [usually goes through the following] stages of: shock; anger; rejection; acceptance; help. (Earley, 1997: 391)

The increased numbers of such schools that can be characterized as 'failing' drew awareness to the issue of school failure. The new inspection system has achieved two things so far. First, it has brought to light the existence of such schools and the nature of their problems. Controversially though, as Stoll and Myers (1998) argue, these schools have always been there, it's just that 'we have been negligent enough to ignore them'. Second, highlighting the problems such schools face by publicly attributing labels of failure has negatively intensified their situation.

Until recently little research has been carried out in the UK explicitly addressing the issue of failing schools and the way to turn them around (Gray and Wilcox, 1995; Barber, 1998; Myers, 1995a; Reynolds, 1991). It has been argued that this reflects the complexity of the differences between these schools, leading consequently to a misinterpretation of appropriate responses (Stoll and Myers, 1998), and indicates the complexity of the concept of failure. As Barber (1998: 19) argues, 'failure in education can be just as catastrophic as failure in the airline industry. It differs only in that it happens more slowly and that no one has yet made the movie.' Therefore, in the study presented next our purpose was to start sketching out this 'movie' by allowing individual voices to be heard.

The study

Recognizing the above arguments, this study set out to enhance understandings of failing schools through a series of illuminative case studies. The investigations were guided by the following research questions:

- What is a failing school's culture like?
- To what extent might the study of cultural factors provide understandings that can help facilitate improvement efforts?
- What are the implications for moving policy and practice forward?

The study began in September 1999. Being fortunate enough, I was allowed entry to four schools in special measures within one English LEA. One of the four schools served the purposes of a pilot study. Having experienced the intensity of the situation in the pilot study school, I anticipated that gaining access to such schools would have been very difficult. Therefore, the other three schools were not randomly selected. Rather they were chosen on the basis of ease of access. All schools shared two common features: they were inner city schools and, moreover, they all were subject to the same LEA policies, services and interventions.

Data collection was carried through to July 2001. During this time, each school was visited on a daily basis for a period of about seven weeks. During these visits evidence was collected through a means of qualitative research methods such as:

- Participant and non-participant observation: observation was the major tool used in gathering information. In all cases the schools and staff were informed of the research purposes. Where it was not possible to proceed with non-participant observation, i.e., in cases where teachers felt uncomfortable with note-taking, I mostly proceeded with participant observation and took part in the process of events during classroom sessions.
- Semi-structured interviews: interviews took place with staff members in the schools, LEA advisers and pupils.
- Unofficial discussions: we also had a range of unofficial discussions with various informants during my visits in these schools.
- Culture activity of the 'Mapping the process of change into schools' project (Ainscow *et al.*, 1995): this activity took the form of a board game and almost all staff took part. It was an opportunity for us to round up my 'impressions' on each school, but it also offered the school staff an opportunity to get together informally and discuss their school culture 'with a view to reaching a group consensus on the three required responses' (see ibid.: 84).

- Documentary analysis: a variety of documents were collected from schools, i.e., staff meetings minutes, school newsletters, brochures, prospectuses, LEA information.

At each stage of the research the schools were given feedback, i.e., after the culture activity, at the end of the visits. Participants were also given written feedback on the interviews we held. This was an opportunity for the 'insiders' to correct, amend or extend it, i.e., to 'subject [the transcription or report] to scrutiny' (Lincoln and Guba, 1985: 314). This stage served as a major and influential step prior to the conceptual part of the data analysis phase and writing up the final draft of the case studies.

Working closely with the data, and having experienced the schools during a troubled period in their lives, it was illustrated that special measures was a very emotional period in the schools' lives, where staff attitudes and beliefs towards their situation influenced their working relationships and impacted on their improvement efforts. Many of the staff did not recognize the severity of their situation and their responsibility in helping to turn it round. Some tended to place responsibility for the school's situation either on other colleagues or the pupils. A few staff were very reluctant to adopt the changes proposed and tended to develop a self-preserving mode: people clung to past practices which provided them with security. Such behaviours were observed particularly in relation to notions of power transition. Many staff were dis-empowered and this, in return, influenced their attitudes towards addressing the key issues that Ofsted highlighted for improvement. In the majority of the cases, it was pointed out, that power transition was felt to be a necessity if the schools were to turn around.

In the three case studies that follow the stories of the study schools unfold. Through these stories, the complexity and uniqueness of each of these schools is illustrated.

Case study 1: 'It will do' vs 'All I want is the best'

They've been in the culture of 'we can make the SATs look good and it doesn't matter about the rest'. They were in the culture of 'the school has got to look good on paper whether the school is good or not'. Now that also reflects on the building ... The previous headteacher was here 20 years. So, that's the problem. They have all been brought up in that culture ... '*it will do*' you know. '*This is ok, this is ok, it will do.*' Not '*all I want is the best*'. They can't understand the situation they are in. Every child is the same in the classroom in their opinion. Even if they are more able or less able, they get the same work. Now, that can't happen. That is

THE problem. It is complacency, and why they haven't been part of any
Education Action Zone, or part of any initiative. (headteacher interview)

St Paul's Primary School was said to be the worst school in the LEA. It is situated
in a well-established ethnic minority community not far from the city centre.
The surrounding area is one of social and economic deprivation. The school is
situated in a valley with an Education Action Zone at both ends. At the time of the
study, the school was part of neither of these.

Staff relationships, even between the established staff, were very fragile and
colleagues did not trust each other; there were several cliques and staff would
criticize and gossip about each other.

Staff were demoralized and at times felt isolated. Working relationships
changed, there was no sharing of good practice and people tended to keep
to themselves, and they were becoming very wary. Some staff seemed to
believe that they were working together as a team, although there was not
much evidence of team behaviour. However, some staff indicated that there
was strong pressure coming from their colleagues regarding the changes
that needed to take place. A number of new staff were brought in to help with
the improvement plans. The majority of the staff were very stressed over the
changes; some characterized themselves as 'old dinosaurs' with reference to
new advances in teaching methods or the use of ICT. Some were unwilling to
adopt the new changes and tended to 'confide' to past practices; at times this
attitude obstructed the school's improvement process since, despite the training
the staff were receiving, there was no consistency in the implementation of the
changes, i.e., target setting and levelling.

Both school and staff seemed to have been caught in a time warp. Most of
the teachers have been in the specific school for an average of 15–20 years.
During this time not many efforts were made to adapt to the current educational
demands and new trends in the educational system as were occurring in the
English educational world. Staff had developed an attitude of self-preserving:
they tried to get on with their work with as little 'interference' from educational
change as possible; they had their own pace and were not much into formalities
and consistency. This attitude particularly seems to have led to complacency.

Complacency and inconsistency had an impact on the pupils. Although
there were no major behavioural problems, the main feeling was that the pupils
did not value education as such. This could also be attributed to the cultural
background of the pupils' families: the majority of the pupils had English as a
second language and in most homes English was not even spoken – a factor that
was an obstacle to the pupils' school performance. There was no punctuality on
behalf of the pupils. In most cases the pupils failed to be on time in the morning
and in most cases failed to do their homework. Also the majority of the pupils did

not wear the school uniform. There was a lack of parental presence in school. As the headteacher explained, this was because in the past the school did not try to embrace parents. Moreover, there were major issues around home violence that led to disruption in the pupils' performance and behaviour.

Another issue for which the school was criticized was the SEN provision; some pupils were on the same stage in the SEN register for 2–3 years. Nevertheless, at the time of my visits the school was trying to build up coherent support for SEN pupils.

Staff believed that it was the LEA's responsibility to help them address their shortcomings with the appropriate support so that they could escape from their 'time warp'. For them the school 'missed out' on the LEA's provisions and stressed that they were forgotten by the LEA. A blaming culture was beginning to form and staff were not very welcoming of the LEA's initiative and training. The LEA teaching staff sent in to support the school were not viewed positively by some of the staff; there was a lot of resentment and ill feeling.

The school had received major criticisms about its leadership and management. The school was reported to have had a poor previous headteacher who was unable to address some of the crucial problems the school faced. Staff believed that the criticisms around the school management had nothing to do with their practice. They failed to realize that this criticism also applied to them and how they managed the curriculum and their class. The coming of the new head was thought as the only solution to the school problems. However, when the new headteacher arrived, a professional with experience in 'failing schools', some staff were very sceptical about her and distanced themselves from her. HMI found the new headteacher to be isolated and the LEA provided her with support at a management level linking her with another headteacher at another school. This was a support strategy that the new headteacher reported to have found very beneficial.

Since the staff were in 'denial' of the correctness of the HMI decision and their situation, staff meetings were at the beginning more headteacher-led. Steadily the headteacher tried to involve the staff more, whenever they were ready to take on more responsibilities. The new headteacher believed that the staff needed to have ownership of the school development and improvement, especially since she would not be with them for long – something she repeatedly made clear to them.

Although staff were kept reasonably well informed of the different changes in school, there were cases where they would see actions being taken without them knowing the reason; for example, the teacher-governor never fed back to them or passed on the governors' meeting minutes. This increased the tension already present in school, worsened staff relationships and created a number of misunderstandings.

People seldom used the staffroom and on very few occasions were all the staff present. The staffroom was a dilapidated, untidy old room bearing great resemblance to the nineteenth-century building it was housed in.

The school buildings were in an appalling state, unsuitable for teaching purposes and some particular areas presented a health hazard. Ofsted had identified the school building as one of the key issues for improvement. The condition of the school buildings was demotivating for both staff and pupils. The existence of two separate buildings also led to staff fragmentation.

Before leaving aside this case for a while, there are a few points that are useful to remember for future thought. We need to bear in mind that what was featured in this school was the deterioration of the school, in terms of both the buildings and the attitudes of people, and the effect all of this had on the development and improvement processes. Such matters were observed in terms of clinging to past practices, fragmented working relationships and a general climate not conducive to change. The story of St Paul's illustrates the significance of the headteacher's role in leading the school out of special measures. Because the headteacher had no previous involvement with the school, she had a clear sense of what the school needed to achieve. However, this raises questions on the sustainability of the improvements once the particular headteacher has left the school. The story also raises a number of questions regarding the LEA-school relationship, and the LEA's responsibilities for preventing one of its schools from reaching this state. Significantly, though, St Paul's is an example of the importance of staff power and the impact their willingness can have on improvement processes.

Case study 2: 'She is not strong enough!'

> She is kind with the children and the staff, but she is most of the time in her office; she is not managing by walking about ... She has many good points, but I don't think she's got strong management skills, or a strong sense of direction. I don't think she knows what she is doing or where we are going. If I was the head I'd say 'this is what I want'. She is not experienced enough for the post she has and I don't think she knows what's happening. She is not experienced enough to deal with these issues adequately. If you've got a supply teacher and you know that the children will play it up, I'd keep popping in. I'd be around for the children to see. But she keeps in her office, so kids know that they'll get away with things ... She is not strong enough. (teacher interview)

Our Souls C.E. Primary School is a voluntary-aided school situated near a city centre. The school is in the middle of a well established, mainly white populated parish, where deprivation factors are very high. The school presented a very vibrant setting with young staff and colourful surroundings. The first impression a visitor would receive on an initial visit to the school would be one of disbelief about the school's situation at the time. Why would a school looking this good, with lively and friendly staff, with 'sensible' pupils, be in special measures?

Staff did not believe that the special measures decision reflected their situation and challenged the Ofsted decision, not getting any pleasure out of it. After the first shock, staff decided to work together to turn their school round; this was a collective decision. Both the staff and the headteacher believed that special measures gave them a sense of urgency in developing and catching up with schools in similar contexts. However, some staff did not believe that their practices had changed very much once in special measures. There was a spirit of collaboration amongst the teachers. This arose mainly because staff seemed to believe that their school needed to develop and improve and also because they were already established as a team. Therefore, collaboration between the staff, i.e., mutual support, sharing of good practice and trust were behaviours naturally exhibited and not imposed on the staff. However, the fact that some of the staff were also friends on a social basis seemed to have impacted on the school's development processes. It appeared that the closeness between them made it difficult to differentiate, at times, from their personal and professional capacities. This was mostly observed in decision-making.

At times there were communication problems between the headteacher and the staff. When building up to an HMI visits, relationships became very tense. In particular the relationship between the headteacher and some of the staff was very fragile. The headteacher was seen to be distant and to spend most of her time in her office, whereas staff would wish to see her practising more 'managing by walking about'. The headteacher was seen to wish to avoid confrontation. At times this gave rise to tension. For example, during a particular staff meeting, a Senior Management Team (SMT) member challenged the headteacher on planning time; this was not to the liking of the headteacher who reported finding this incident threatening and called the specific SMT member to her office for a private word. Such an attitude possibly led to mistrust between the staff; there was serious talk going on behind the headteacher's back. This led to communication problems. Although it was shown that decision-making was done on a collaborative level between staff and the headteacher, the majority of the decisions remained with the headteacher and this created some issues in working relationships in the school. On occasions she was defensive of her staff and school. It was considered that the headteacher was promoted in this job at a very early stage in her career and at times she was characterized as too inexperienced to do this job, hence the defensiveness. Staff believed that their headteacher was weak, and would welcome another headteacher or a deputy headteacher who would put things into perspective for them. It was expressed that the school lacked a sense of direction and a clear vision for its future. This brought stress and tension in school.

The staff visited the staffroom constantly, which was a happy place to be in. Despite the fact that the majority of the staff were seen to believe in the collaborative working relationships they had established, there was a subtle division between Key Stages. There was the impression that Key Stage 1 shared resentment for having to go through the whole process of special measures since the major criticism lay with Key Stage 2. However, when it came to making decisions for the school's improvement programme and its future, most of the staff were seen to put aside any differences they had.

The school blamed the LEA for not supporting as much as they should have done. There was criticisms of the competence of the LEA staff sent to help the school. With reference to the LEA support, the headteacher stressed at times that being in special measures made no difference in the LEA support that the school received; she added that she still had to fight for the support promised to them whereas it was expected that support would be coming in plentifully in various 'guises'.

The school had achieved good improvements during their HMI visits; however, it did not seem to have the spark needed to successfully turn around a special measures school. It was argued that the school would come out of special measures, however, not a much better school than when it went in.

This account reinforces the significance of collaboration as an improvement strategy particularly in schools which face such challenging circumstances. In particular, though, this account raises questions about the role of the headteacher. Clearly, the school needed a change of its existing culture. However, the resistance the school seemed to exhibit in adopting changes may have been characterized by the fact that its headteacher was the one who took the school into special measures. The case of Our Souls raises the issue of keeping the existing headteacher during a period of reform. On the other hand, if a new headteacher was brought in the school, would the improvement process be facilitated or would problems of a different nature appear? The story of this school indicates the need for intensive support at a management level for those who have leading roles in schools in special measures.

Case study 3: The two staffrooms

> We need one staffroom, where people are talking and sharing and support each other, not this. (headteacher interview)

St Barbara's C.E. Primary School is situated in a well-established inner city community; the majority of the inhabitants have Afro-Caribbean origins. The school premises are particularly well developed and did not provide grounds for Ofsted to point them out as an improvement issue. The school premises used to be part of another school that previously closed because of special measures. The school had two separate staffrooms: one smoking and one non-smoking. What was significant was the fact that these two rooms physically facilitated a culture of division in the school.

Staff gradually started to recognize the reasons that the school had gone into special measures. However, there was still some denial of their actual situation and the extent of their responsibility for this. At the time of my visits there was a blaming culture in school. Staff tended to attribute blame for their situation on the fact that they moved premises, only six weeks prior to Ofsted, and on their new headteacher and the changes he had brought in school. A conspiracy theory notion had soon developed. Some staff seemed to believe that the inspectors had reached their final decision after reading the school's development plans that the new headteacher had drawn up after being in the school only six weeks prior to Ofsted. It was argued that the development plan was misleading since it indicated that there were weaknesses in the school and issues that needed to be addressed; these, some staff felt, did not reflect reality. However, the new headteacher believed that the reason why some of the staff failed to see what the reality was, was the fact that they were part of it for so many years. Therefore, they could not be as self-critical and objective as the new headteacher could be since he had no history of prior involvement with the school. This seems to have brought resentment on behalf of some members of staff, which was a potential danger to the school's improvement process. Staff who were unwilling to adapt to the changes the school needed had either made a conscious decision to leave school or were eased out.

With staff turnover, a 'them and us' culture was created. The established staff and the new staff were seen to work and liase in isolation. This notional division was also increased by the physical division in school, hence the two separate staffrooms. The established staff would only go to the smoking staffroom (whether they smoked or not) and the new staff to the non-smoking staffroom. The resentment was mostly directed towards the LEA staff who were often called 'super-teachers'. Resentment and division increased particularly since the headteacher seemed to be inclined to believe more in the power of those in the non-smoking staffroom. This 'them and us' culture and division led to communi-cation problems and affected working relationships and decision-making.

At times there was direct confrontation between staff members and hard words were exchanged. Criticism and inappropriate language was used in the smoking staffroom, mostly directed towards the headteacher and the 'super-teachers'. Established staff argued that they felt undervalued and that their contributions to the school were not acknowledged. At times the smoking staffroom was a very sad place to be in and deterioration was obvious. The other staffroom had gradually become a happier place; there was more laughter and more contact between the staff who visited it. This was acknowledged by the staff who saw laughter as a sign of improvement and an indication of the changing culture.

For some of the established staff who had gone along with the changes there was an issue of loyalty towards their colleagues. They seemed to believe that some of their colleagues were treated unprofessionally. This made it harder for them to work alongside those who were seen to be disrespectful to their colleagues.

Consistency was an issue in school, on behalf of both the teachers and the pupils. Since some staff did not believe in the changes, they did not necessarily implement what was proposed, i.e., the new discipline and behaviour policies. However, on a daily basis not all staff adopted what was proposed and tended to openly disagree and 'mock' this initiative; 'we know these children and there is no way that this is going to work', some tended to say.

Pupils' behaviour was an important issue in school. There were major outbreaks in classrooms, fights in the playgrounds and children leaving school without permission.

The headteacher was a very determined person and had managed to make the school governors agree to close down the smoking staffroom; he believed the staff needed to be together and added that the culture in the smoking staffroom endangered the school's improvement efforts. His vision for the school was to become a vehicle for bringing about significant improvements in the development of the broader community. He was trying to establish a new culture in school by being around, constantly reminding people of things to come and reinforcing positive behaviour.

However, it was argued that the communication problems in school reflected a lack on the headteacher's part. Nonetheless there were examples of bottom up lack of communication as well. For example, one day there was an incident in school where pupils were pretending to be buying and selling drugs. The deputy headteacher attended to the matter since the headteacher was not in school at the time. A week later during an interview with the headteacher I tried to find out more information about this incident. To my surprise the headteacher knew nothing of this matter.

It was also argued that the LEA had not actually helped the school with the move or helped to postpone Ofsted. Some staff were very critical of the LEA, arguing that they have not been actively present in the school in modelling lessons, sharing good practice or supporting them.

The case of St Barbara's illustrates the tension arising at the micro-political level of the school. This is an example of the significance of power as a lever for bringing about change and influencing improvement. Also, there was an increased tension in school between the need for development and the need to maintain some of their existing character and features; tension was increased with the transfer of power to those who were more prone to change. Power transition led to a culture of division. Such tension was seen to impact on the development processes in the school. This had implications for the role of the headteacher. He was aware of the tension arising in school and the implications it had on its development progress. However, as he stressed, what had to come first was the interest of the pupils. This case also raises questions about the role of the LEA; this links with the debate on the current reform agenda about the role of LEAs.

Perspectives from the inside: emergent themes

There are a number of themes emerging from these three case studies concerning the impact that special measures had on each schools' cultures. The three case studies also raise a number of implications for improvement efforts.

Attitudes

We all frequently talk about our own and other people's attitudes in an effort to understand the exhibited behaviour and its impact on the world around us. As Fishbein and Ajzen (1975) argue, attitudes are 'learned predispositions to respond in a consistently favourable or unfavourable way towards a given object, person, or event'.

In the analysis of the schools' cultures it was observed that staff attitudes and perceptions towards their situation were impacting negatively on the improvement efforts and delayed the development pace. It was observed that most of the staff in the schools had gone, or were still going, through what might be described as a culture of denial and refused to acknowledge the reality of their situation. Steadily a blaming culture was created in which staff tended to hold either other colleagues or the pupils responsible for being made subject to special measures. A common characteristic in such situations is to stress that ' "they" are pushing new ideas down our throat' as Stoll and Fink also pointed out (1998: 196). The rejection and denial of the decision and the re-directing of blame was in some degree led by a defensiveness towards the 'threatening messages' (Reynolds, 1991: 101) the schools said to have been receiving from the outside.

The analysis of the schools' cultures showed an overall reluctance on behalf of some staff members towards change. To some extent the changes were seen to be 'ego-endangering' (Rosenholtz, 1989: 6). Some staff found themselves deeply 'stuck' into the culture of special measures. As a result, they found it difficult to dig themselves out of the negativism and pessimism they were found in. Going along with the changes contradicted what they have come to take for granted over the years: their 'reality defining' concept (Hargreaves, 1995). It can be argued that 'clinging' to past practice (Reynolds, 1991) is culturally oriented, as it refers to a school's 'deep history' (Louis and Miles, 1990: 187) and can, therefore, bring barriers to change (ibid.). As Schein (1972: 75) argues:

> The change agent must assume that the members of the system will be committed to their present ways of operating and will, therefore, resist learning something new. As a consequence the *essence* of a planned change process is the unlearning of present ways of doing things. It is felt to be in this *unlearning* process that most of the difficulties of planned change arise.

In the reality of special measures, many staff reported feeling 'useless' and 'a failure'; in particular, some stressed that they felt they had failed their pupils and added that they did not deserve this. Being in special measures was a very emotional time for the schools and their staff. What was present in all schools was the initial disappointment felt with the announcement of the decision; staff generally said that they felt de-motivated in continuing to work and expressed feelings of discontent and lack of confidence:

> To be honest I go to pieces when someone comes in. I just knew that you were going to come in today, and I didn't like the idea. I go to pieces when anyone comes in ... the Ofsted experience was tremendous and did not do much good for my confidence. I am now trying to get my confidence back, to get my belief back that I can do the job. I'm working on several strategies for doing this, as I do not have the time to build up the experience needed. I have been drained. Although HMI has been a constructive experience in a way, Ofsted had damaged me as far as I am concerned ... since then I've had no confidence in my teaching. In fact I am going home every night crying my eyes out. (teacher interview)

And also:

> I just want my life back; my children and my husband ... because there are so many things to do and you don't have the time for it, and when you are a perfectionist like myself you devote so much more time ... I'm happy here; at least I was. (teacher conversation)

Staff also expressed disappointment about their educational authority and its lack of support. In this sense, the schools could be characterized as survivalist. As Hargreaves (1995) argues, in such schools teachers feel unsupported both by their headteacher and by their colleagues. The LEA teaching staff, LEA advisers or newly appointed staff were often referred to as 'the saviours' (teacher interview); such comments often had a sarcastic tone attach to them. Often a 'them and us' culture was initiated. Some staff were seen to be very critical of the suggestions or contributions of the new members of staff and/or the LEA advisers.

Relationships

Both working and personal relationships were very tense and, at times, counter-productive. The pressure felt appeared to make staff at the schools less cohesive. What appeared to keep some of these people together was their previous shared experiences and their shared cultural assumptions, i.e., 'the way we used to do things'. The change in working styles and staff had created a conspiracy theory notion amongst some of the staff, who were observed to be prejudiced against their new colleagues. According to Hayes (1995: 119), being prejudiced is an attitude applied 'to a target regardless of the target's own individuality or nature'. For example, in one of the schools a headteacher stressed:

> The irony is, I think that I am actually good at supporting staff, but that won't be their [established staff] perception. (headteacher interview)

Such attitudes were seen to foster a division between the staff members and emphasize the 'them and us' culture that had formed. Some members of staff characteristically called such culture as 'the forming of a "nucleus"', when referring to cliques:

> Since special measures cohesiveness has eroded ... they [the headteacher and the new staff] have created a nucleus, which we [the established staff] are not part of ... they tend to keep things to themselves. (teacher interview)

Staff were seen to be working in isolation and were very wary of people. In all schools a form of what Hargreaves (1994) named as 'balkanization' existed. Regardless of the form which balkanization took, the majority of the teachers were seen to be part of a group, whether that was the group of the established staff, the new staff, a key stage staff group or the staff versus the headteacher. For example, this resentment let some staff at St Barbara's ask 'are we having a third staffroom now?' (teacher comment) on seeing some people working closely together to the exclusion of other staff members. This seemed to increase tension and possibly initiate conflict. Apart from the pressure put on staff from HMI, the LEA and the headteacher, what also brought about conflict in school were the individuals' own agendas. Some staff felt that their professional development was not taken into account and they were sidelined by the special measures situation.

As Ball (1987: 32) argues, since innovations are not neutral, they will bring about tension and conflict, and if we wish to introduce changes or propose any innovation, this has to be 'in relation to immediate interests and concerns of those members [who are] likely to be affected, directly or indirectly [by change]'. This frustration was also increased by the fact that some staff believed that the 'improvements' that had been taking place in school were 'rush jobs' and 'window dressing'.

Power transition

A source of tension was the fact that some staff in these schools were dis-empowered. Power was transferred, most of the time, to the headteacher, and often to the new people coming in. In most situations this was not to the liking of many of the staff in the schools and was often linked with demotivation, lack of confidence and feelings of worthlessness.

The phenomenon of power transition, and the tension it can give rise to was most evident at St Barbara's:

> That's where the power is lying now [non-smoking staffroom], that's [the smoking staffroom] where the change is, and that's [the smoking staffroom] where power used to lie and it was a negative power ... I know that there are people who will take the dislike of me to the grave, that won't still spit on me in a desert in 20 years' time. That's the reality ... I've taken the ball away and I won't let them play the game they wanted to play. (headteacher interview)

However, what was observed in St Paul's particularly was the fact that the headteacher gradually distributed power to the staff members. At times the headteacher reminded the staff that she would not be with them for long as her contract was only for five terms. With this in mind she stressed to the staff that if they wished to see their school moving forward, they needed to have ownership of its improvement initiatives. Staff gradually begun to realize this; the first sign of this change was in the way staff meetings were held.

Contradictory to the other two schools, Our Souls presented some peculiarity. There the power still lay with the existing headteacher. Her observed defensiveness was seen to obstruct the school's improvement efforts and increased the resentment already felt by many in the staff team.

Ball (1987: 19, emphasis in original) characterizes schools as 'arenas of struggle', which are 'driven with actual or potential conflict between members'. In the situation, therefore, of schools in special measures, the potential of such a struggle is more intensified by the pressures exercised over the transition of power which most of the times helped in the creation of 'allies' and 'enemies':

> When you are doing what I am doing you should not expect to make friends, but enemies, because people don't like to hear the truth ... I won't take sides but staff in crisis always want you to take their side. (headteacher interview)

Leadership

'Leadership is currently in vogue', Harris (2003) characteristically points out. This renewed emphasis on improving leadership capacity and capabilities stems from the need to cope with accelerated educational change and development. Leadership has been widely acknowledged amongst the majority of the countries in the Western world as the lead component in educational effectiveness and the need to raise standards.

Although this study did not begin as a study of leadership, leadership was one of the emergent themes; its importance was highlighted in all the schools. One of the significant matters emphasized by the headteachers was the belief that all children can learn and succeed. Added to that was the headteachers' concern about their pupils' welfare. On a number of occasions the headteacher of St Barbara's had left school with another member of staff to look for pupils who had run away from school. As the particular headteacher stressed:

> But I'm not here firstly for the staff, but for the pupils. I'm here secondly for the staff. (headteacher interview)

Another factor that characterized the headteachers' behaviour was their commitment to facilitating effective communication, building a community and establishing ownership of a shared culture. As the headteacher of St Paul's stressed:

> It is pointless not to involve the staff because if at the end this school stays open, I won't be here. They have to learn to stand on their own feet. (headteacher interview)

And also:

> We have reached the point where I [the headteacher] was slowly withdrawing my intensive 'I do everything' type, because that's not helping them. So, the change we've made is in the way we run staff meetings ... So they all have an input now ... It's passing the ownership from me to the school as a sound practice. (headteacher interview)

What came to be the foundation for the initiation of such behaviours was the fact that the headteachers were clear-sighted and had a vision for their school:

> I want us to be in a situation where as a vibrant, successful part of this community we are actually beginning to have an influence and an impact beyond the narrow education issues. (headteacher interview)

However, at Our Souls the headteacher was being criticized for not being a visionary leader. This brought about tension and frustration amongst her staff:

> She [the headteacher] sometimes fails to hear the staff and the signals we send out to her. For example, with the planning. The planning was too much and we all moaned about it. When we strongly said 'Planning: no more', she turned round and said 'Oh dear, is it starting to bother you'. Sometimes she is not clear-sighted and this has to do with the fact that she is not around the school premises much, rather she stays in her office most of the times. (teacher interview)

The pressure and the tension special measures brought about to the school culture could be strongly detected. The headteachers were called to manage this tension and any problems directly related to the uniqueness of their context. They were often faced with unpredictability and conflict, and their interpersonal skills were called upon many a times. This indicated that one of the 'requirements' of a headteacher in schools in special measures is to be people-centred and provide moral support to the members of the school community as and when its needed. In this sense the headteachers' leadership style and capabilities helped to form a notion of 'social capital' (Hargreaves, 2003) through the investment in, and development of, others.

It is important here to note that in three of the schools in this study (including the pilot school), the headteachers were brought in by the LEA in order to help the schools in their improvement and development efforts, as they were considered to be experts for the job. As one of the LEA officers stated, bringing in a headteacher

> without any package [is far more effective]. They will have a job to do [and that is] to take the school out of special measures ... This is the school,

as it was, and this is the school as it's going to be, and not arguing on the decision, they [the staff] just have to accept that. (LEA officer interview)

Whilst the headteachers that were brought in had no previous package with the school and could be more strict and focused, some of them also pointed out that because of this they intimidated the staff:

> Yes I do [intimidate the staff]. I know I do. Now, it is because usually they are a lazy lot and somebody has to 'crack the whip'. Even if 'crack the whip' says 'look if you don't get your finger out, we're going to close this school, and I can always find a job in schools that have problems, can you find another job?' (headteacher interview)

This raises a very important issue: that of sustainability. Whilst the schools may come out of special measures, we cannot give any informed judgement as to the potential for longer-term growth and this is inextricably linked with the fact that the headteachers who will facilitate the improvement programme will most probably leave the schools right after special measures is removed. The fact that the staff knew that this was possible, at times increased the insecurity and instability they felt. The situation to them seemed to be merely 'a quick fix'.

As argued elsewhere (Nicolaidou, 2002; West *et al.*, 2003; Ainscow *et al.*, 2003) the issue of sustainability remains a challenge. In these respects, further discussion needs to take place as to what forms of longer-term support is needed for schools in challenging circumstances and, in particular, those under special measures. This leads me to think that those who are proving support to these schools, i.e., LEAs, government officials, will need to reconsider and design longer-term strategies that will facilitate and sustain improvement efforts in schools in special measures. In the case of new headteachers being brought in, I believe that such approaches need to have a more detailed plan for the disengagement of this support as many of the people in the schools I visited were becoming increasingly insecure by the mere fact that support offered to them, i.e., human and financial resources, would be withdrawn once special measures were removed.

Reflections

The case studies illustrate a number of important considerations in supporting schools in special measures and providing sustainable improvement.

Study of local practices

The study (see Nicolaidou, 2002) has illustrated that each of the schools visited was 'unhappy in its own way' (*Anna Karenina*, Leo Tolstoy). Nonetheless, what they seemed to have in common was the influence their history had on their culture and how their cultures and structures interacted, impacting on (and developing) relationships, attitudes, feelings and actions. Although the schools were all made subject to special measures and there were a number of features present to all of them, one can still argue on the uniqueness of each case. This leads to the conclusion that it is through the careful study of local practices, in relation to their contexts (Ainscow, 1998), that we can proceed to make suggestions for future development. By understanding practices in relation to cultures, i.e., how people think and interact, we can then learn to appreciate how peoples' own interests may become an obstacle to development. What the case studies suggest is that the schools needed to take into consideration such matters when trying to establish their 'new' ways of working.

This would then facilitate 'participation' and, in this way, people would be motivated to make changes for themselves. It has been widely argued that school success ultimately depends on teachers' success in their classroom; and teachers work better and more efficiently once they have the opportunity to collaborate, share ideas, receive and offer support from and to their peers. Teacher collaboration has been recognized as a vital factor for successful school improvement and change (Fullan, 1991). In particular, as Fullan argues, the power for change lies within effective collaboration.

Therefore, participation and more collaborative ways of working need to be necessary features of any improvement process in any school in special measures. Often collaboration in a school is measured by the degree of communication, mutual support and peer learning. Collaborative cultures are seen to be most compatible with development and improvement efforts. Nonetheless, in many schools in special measures collaboration mechanisms are hardly in place to allow for teachers to work together. Teachers are not seen to be encouraged, nor do they have the time and space available to work alongside their colleagues, considering the increasing demands placed on them with the special decision and also by the current educational policies and changes. Thus, they are rather found to be working in isolation and feel threatened and sometimes alienated from the rest of the staff team. I believe, however, that the biggest challenge of getting teachers to work together is not a technological problem, but rather a cultural and organizational one, and has implications for the role of the headteacher as the school leader.

Leadership functions and organizational culture

The research evidence presented in the case studies, clearly reveal how the headteachers' leadership styles influence school life and how they impact on school culture. The impact on school culture is best seen as a reaction of the teachers towards the leadership style adopted by their headteacher (Blase and Anderson, 1995). Reflecting on the case studies reinforces such an argument.

Although much has been argued about which style of leadership best facilitates organizational change, I am left feeling that no one particular form of leadership style can work best in schools in special measures. In the particular schools the headteachers' leadership style ranged from being over-directive and prescriptive, to sharing power and being democratic. Crucially the case study schools indicated that their approach to leadership had been a flexible and 'reflexive' (Southworth, 1998) one. Their behaviour should be influenced by what they are trying to achieve and how well their propositions will be accepted by their followers. The data illustrate that leadership is both influenced by and impacts on its followers' sub-cultures. In the accounts presented, the headteachers' behaviour seemed related to some of the staff members' willingness to adopt the changes. The study indicated that unless the staff were willing to accept suggestions for improvement, there was little that the headteachers could do, not denying, though, that 'without the [headteachers'] support, there is little scope for others to make a contribution' (Wallace, 2002: 166).

Three of the four headteachers of the schools in the study were brought in either just before the schools went into special measures or soon after in order to 'turn them round'. In one sense what the LEA had tried to do in these schools was to bring in hero-innovators:

> This then is the myth of the hero-innovator: the idea that you can produce, by training, a knight in shining armour who, loins girded with new technology and beliefs, will assault his organisational fortress and institute changes both in himself and others at a stroke. Such a view is ingenuous.
> (Georgiades and Phillimore, 1975: 315)

Nowadays more and more responsibility is being placed onto headteachers in England and Wales, but with less time and, in most cases, less support. The study indicates that the headteachers cannot address such situations alone since 'the fact of the matter is that organisations such as schools and hospitals will, like dragons, eat hero-innovators for breakfast' (ibid.). The headteachers in this study were seen to be struggling to achieve their tasks, and even HMI found them to be isolated and signalled that there must be better ways of supporting these headteachers. Consequently, it is argued that there is a need to foster partnerships at the leadership level. In the schools in this study, the headteachers were linked with other headteachers, or educational consultants; the headteachers agreed how productive this had been for them and their schools. However, they argued that such initiatives should have been better facilitated. Our experience in another project on schools in challenging circumstances (Ainscow *et al.*, 2002a, b), in a different LEA, reinforces the case for leadership support networks in the shape of 'school-to-school inter-dependence' (ibid). In this particular project collaboration has been extended to facilitated both institutional and individual level cooperation, whereby a group of schools, their headteachers and staff were brought together with a view to foster improvement.

The question remains on why hero-innovators such as the super-heads fail, i.e., headteachers in Fresh-start schools. As Reynolds (1991) remarked in a study that failed to turn around ineffective schools, the schools' internal conditions, their culture, may have been inappropriately ignored. In the same way we can argue that the schools' 'fabric' was inappropriately ignored by the 'superheads' concept. If we accept that leadership connects with notions of organization, groups (followers), objectives, tasks, motivation, facilitating efforts, provision of resources, relationships and teamwork, then we can argue that leadership is about organizational cultures and bringing about organizational change (Hitt, 1988). Leadership and culture, as Schein (1972) argues, are two sides of the same coin when examined closely, and neither can be understood by itself. Therefore, changes that detach one from the other and disregard the relationship between leadership and culture are likely to fail. The headteacher then in a school in special measures will need to be seen as a change agent facilitating the creation of a new culture:

> You are breaking up fixed ways of thinking and working; you're breaking a culture, an educational culture in order to create a new one. (headteacher interview)

Added to the above, the case studies illustrated the need for the headteachers to be 'multilingual':

> School [headteachers] will need to be 'multilingual', working within multiple and competing discourses e.g. of managerialism and care, account-ability and professional autonomy, competition and collaboration, personal and social education, needs of students and the narrow instrumentalism of government required 'standards'. (Gewirtz *et al.*, 1995)

The LEA

The study of these schools in special measures points to the importance of support that LEAs can provide to the schools. There was an increased request for support from the LEA despite the blaming culture initiated towards LEA provision. As Derrington (2000) notes in his study on the contributions of LEAs in school improvement, the majority of the schools indicated that they needed the LEA support in order to improve.

The roles of English LEAs need to be revisited since their powers have been reduced with the current reform agenda in England and Wales; consequently the support they offered to their schools and particularly to schools in special measures has been hindered. The evidence of this study shows that in order for the schools to focus their efforts on the pressing objective of raising standards and having special measures removed, there was a strong reliance on the LEA to provide a wide range of support at a management level as well as at a teaching level. The schools welcomed LEA support; none of them said that they could proceed with substantial improvements without the help and guidance of the LEA. Nevertheless, some within the particular schools felt that the LEA's lack of action had contributed to their problem. Does the LEA, therefore, have the credibility to take on the tasks necessary in order to help the schools? Acknowledging that 'the role of LEAs is not to control schools, but to challenge all schools to improve and support those which need help to raise standards' (DfEE, 1997: 67), then how can an LEA know that there are problems unless it is closely involved within its schools? Of course, it is important to recognize that the balance between prevention of problems and intervention after problems occur is a difficult one to strike. However, there does seem to be evidence of a reaction from officers in some English LEAs against the perceived pressure to stay out of schools unless they are known to be failing. For example, as part of its prepara- tions for a recent visit of Ofsted, another LEA noted: 'This LEA, whilst recognising the parameters of the new relationship between schools and LEAs, set out by the DfEE ... must also fulfil its wider role of securing improvement in all its schools ... **Prevention is better, and less expensive, than intervention**' (bold in original, Nicolaidou *et al.*, 2001).

Commentary

I was fortunate to experience part of the lives of four schools in special measures. In this chapter I only present a partial view of the lives of such schools. However, this report has provided vivid accounts of the situa- tions these schools face that were not extensively available because entry to such schools was usually restricted by the intensity of special measures. Inside observations of these very sensitive settings allow us to say that where improvement efforts have failed it is because it is thought that such schools are faced with predictable and straightforward problems. On the contrary. My understandings of such schools indicate that they are faced with complex and unique issues and that no one best solution will serve all. However, I am left feeling that such situations depend very much on the nature of the leadership. Leadership functions in schools in special measures must focus on creating the conditions for school improvement, i.e., restoring the schools' internal capacities for renewal through facilitating positive and collaborative working relationships, team building, creating a new culture and establishing shared ownership, whilst having an impact on the broader community.

References

Ainscow, M. (1998) 'Reaching out to all learners: some lessons from experience'. Paper presented at the International Conference on School Effectiveness and School Improvement, Manchester, UK.

Ainscow, M., Hargreaves, D. and Hopkins, D. (1995) 'Mapping the process of change in schools: the development of six new research techniques', *Evaluation and Research in Education*, 9, 2, 75–90.

Ainscow, M., Nicolaidou, M. and West, M. (2003) 'Supporting schools in difficulties: a study of the role of school-to-school cooperation', *TOPIC*, NfER.

Ainscow, M., Nicolaidou, M. and West, M. (2002a) 'Supporting schools in difficulties: a study of the role of school-to-school cooperation'. Paper Present at the BERA 2002 Conference, Exeter, UK.

Ainscow, M., Nicolaidou, M. and West, M. (2002b) *Working Together for School Improvement: An Evaluation of the Kingsdown Partnership Project*. http://www.man.ac.uk/leadership/resources.htm#papers

Ball, S. J. (1987) *The Micro-Politics of the School: Towards a Theory of School Organisation*. London: Routledge.

Barber, M. (1998) 'The Dark Side of the Moon: imagining an end to failure in urban education', in L. Stoll and K. Myers (eds) *No Quick Fixes*. London: Falmer Press.

Blase, J. and Anderson, G. (1995) *The Micropolitics of Educational Leadership*. London: Cassell.

Derrington, C. (2000) *The LEA Contribution to School Improvement – A Role Worth Fighting For*. London: NFER.

DfEE (1997) *White Paper: Excellence in Schools.* London: The Stationery Office.

Earley, P. (1997) 'External inspections, "failing schools" and the role of governing bodies', *School Leadership and Management*, 17, 3, 387–400.

Fishbein, M. and Ajzen, I. (1975) *Attitude Intention and Behaviour: An Introduction to Theory and Research.* Reading, MA: Addison-Wesley.

Fullan, M. (1991) *The New Meaning of Educational Change.* London: Cassell.

Georgiades, N. J. and Phillimore, L. (1975) 'The myth of the hero-innovator: alternative strategies for organisational change', in C. C. Kernan and F. P. Woodford (eds) *Behaviour Modification with the Severely Retarded.* Amsterdam: Elsevier.

Gewirtz, S., Ball, S. J. and Bowe, R. (1995) *Market, Choice and Education in Education.* Buckingham: Open University Press.

Gray, J. and Hannon, V. (1996) 'HMI's Interpretations of schools' examination results', *Journal of Educational Policy*, 1, 23–33.

Gray, J. and Wilcox, B. (1995) 'The challenge of turning round ineffective schools', in J. Gray and B. Wilcox (eds) *Good School, Bad School.* Buckingham: Open University Press.

Hargreaves, A. (1994) *Changing Teachers, Changing Times.* London: Cassell.

Hargreaves, D. (1995) 'School culture, school effectiveness and school improvement', *School Effectiveness and School Improvement*, 6, 91, 23–46.

Hargreaves, D. (2003) 'From Improvement to Transformation'. Keynote speech, International Congress for School Effectiveness and Improvement 2003, Sydney, Australia.

Harris, A. (2003) 'The changing context of leadership: research, theory and practice', in A. Harris, C. Day, D. Hopkins, M. Hadfiled, A. Hargreaves and C. Chapman (eds), *Effective Leadership for School Improvement.* London: Routledge.

Hayes, N. (1995) *Principles of Social Psychology.* Hove, UK: Lawrence Erlbaum Associates.

Hitt, W. D. (1988) *The Leader Manager.* Columbus, OH: Battelle Press.

Lincoln, Y. and Guba, E. (1985) *Naturalistic Inquiry.* Thousand Oaks, CA: Sage

Louis, K. S. and Miles, M. B. (1990) *Improving the Urban High School.* New York: Teachers College Press.

Myers, K. (1995) 'Intensive Care for the Chronically Sick'. Paper presented at the Conference for Educational Research, University of Bath, UK.

Myers, K. and Goldstein, H. (1998) 'Who's failing?', in L. Stoll and K. Myers (eds), *No Quick Fixes*. London: Falmer Press.

Nicolaidou, M. (2002) 'Understanding failing schools: perspectives from the inside'. Unpublished PhD, The University of Manchester.

Nicolaidou, M., Ainscow, M. and Howes, A. (2001) 'Making sense of the role of English Local Education Authorities in relation to failing schools'. Paper presented at the International Congress on School Effectiveness and Improvement. Toronto, Canada

Reynolds, D. (1991) 'Changing ineffective schools', in M. Ainscow (ed.) *Effective Schools for All*. London: Fulton.

Rosenholtz, S. (1989) *Teachers' Workplace: The Social Organisation of Schools*. New York: Longman.

Schein, E. (1972) *Professional Education: Some New Directions*. New York: McGraw-Hill.

Southworth, G. (1998) *Leading Improving Primary School: The Work of Headteachers and Deputy Heads*. London: Falmer Press.

Stoll, L. and Fink, D. (1998) 'The cruising school: the unidentified ineffective school', in L. Stoll and K. Myers (eds) *No Quick Fixes*. London: Falmer Press.

Stoll, L. and Myers, K. (1998) *No Quick Fixes*. London: Falmer Press.

Wallace, M. (2002). 'Modelling distributed leadership and management effectiveness: primary school senior management teams in England and Wales', *School Effectiveness and School Improvement*, 13, 2, 163–86.

West, M., Ainscow, M. and Nicolaidou, M. (2003) 'Putting our heads together'. Paper presented at the International Congress for School Effectiveness and Improvement 2003, Sydney, Australia.

Winkley, D. (1999) 'An examination of Ofsted', in C. Cullingford (ed.) *An Inspector Calls*. London: Kogan Page Limited.

5 Some Issues and Problems in Evaluating Changes and Improvements in 'Low-Performing' Schools

John Gray

CHAPTER OVERVIEW

The measure of school performance has always been a contested issue. The form of measure of performance for those schools in challenging circumstances is particularly troubling, as they are clearly unlike the more effective schools. In this chapter the author questions the appropriacy of the current performance measurement suggesting it is based on 'inappropriate yardsticks'. In so doing, he opens to question the current concept of school development, how it is perceived and reported and more widely understood through existing measures. He argues that in its existing form the performance measure fails to provide sufficient context specificity and, as a result, the formative value of the measurement data is reduced in effect. The reality of schools in difficult circumstances is such that small often difficult to measure effects begin to accumulate and bear fruits over longer time frames than those currently in use. As we begin to be able to define the characteristics of successful intervention in schools in difficult circumstances in ways such as deepening levels of sharing of pedagogic skill and knowledge, there are some signs that we might also begin to model and more effectively utilize revised performance measures.

Introduction

There is increasing interest, on both sides of the Atlantic, in tackling the problem of so-called 'low-performing' schools. In this chapter I consider some of the strategies that have been (and might be) employed to identify such schools as well as some of the problems associated with understanding how they might be helped to improve. Part of my argument will be that the difficulties such exercises throw up have been underestimated. In short, a greater degree of sensitivity to the challenges schools in such circumstances face is probably required.

Underlying my concern is a wider debate, which has been rumbling on for much of the past decade, about whether the dominant paradigms for evaluating school quality and improvement are appropriate for schools of all types. The danger, of course, of arguing for a different approach is that one risks reinforcing any latent tendency on the part of the educationally advantaged to dismiss the efforts of schools which serve others less favourably placed. Before opting for different evaluative frameworks, therefore, closer scrutiny of existing approaches is required.

Issues of identification: a clash of perspectives

Two different models or approaches are currently in play with respect to public judgements of school performance. What I term 'Model 1' is based on what is commonly called a 'standards-based' approach. Essentially, all schools are judged against a single yardstick such as the percentages of pupils securing five or more A*–C passes. The model takes little or no account of context.

The assumptions underlying Model 2 are based on a 'value-added' approach. This model takes into account pupils' starting points and tries to identify the contributions schools make to their pupils' progress over time. Sometimes additional variables, related to social context and other factors known to affect pupil progress, are built into the analysis with a view to creating as close a series of comparisons between schools serving 'similar' pupil populations as possible.

Table 5.1 brings the two models together into a single framework. It is based on the assumption that, within Model 1, roughly one-fifth of the schools are performing at levels which are 'high' in comparison with national averages, one-fifth are 'low' and the remainder are performing at or around national levels and are therefore 'average'. Obviously these groupings could be varied to meet different assumptions. The same assumption is then made with respect to Model 2 with the same cut-offs: in one-fifth of the schools, pupils are making considerably more progress than would be predicted from knowledge of their starting points, in one-fifth considerably less and in the remainder progress is around what would be expected. Based on the assumption that there are 100 schools in the table, the numbers falling into each cell of the table are also indicated.

It is immediately clear that this procedure produces a clash of perspectives with respect to the numbers of schools which might be classified as 'causing concern'. Model 1 identifies 20 schools as coming into the 'low' performance category. By contrast, Model 2 identifies only four of the 20 (see cell 9 of Table 5.1) as falling well below what might reasonably be expected. The performances of the remaining 16 (in cells 7 and 8) are

Table 5.1: Two models for identifying schools which might be causing concern

	Model 2 High Pupil Progress	Model 2 Average Pupil Progress	Model 2 Low Pupil Progress	Total
Model 1 High Pupil Standards	(1) 4 schools	(2) 12 schools	(3) 4 schools	20 schools
Model 1 Average Pupil Standards	(4) 12 schools	(5) 36 schools	(6) 12 schools	60 schools
Model 1 Low Pupil Standards	(7) 'Problem' school for Model 1, not for Model 2 4 schools	(8) 'Problem' school for Model 1, not for Model 2 12 schools	(9) 'Problem' school for Model 1 and Model 2 4 schools	20 schools
Total	20 schools	60 schools	20 schools	100 schools

not seen as problematic. Indeed, four of the schools are judged, given their intakes, to be making a considerable contribution to their pupils' progress (see cell 7), over and above what might reasonably have been expected. These are schools which would probably be judged to be succeeding 'despite the odds'.

Understanding and reinterpreting 'contexts'

'Disadvantage', in educational terms, can take many forms. Poverty, broken homes, lack of familiarity with the dominant language, ethnicity and special educational needs are amongst those most frequently referred to, not least because they have shown up across countless surveys as correlates of 'low performance'. None, however, can be interpreted unproblematically, partly because of changing circumstances and partly because of changes in the assumptions upon which evaluation models are perched.

Eligibility for (and/or take up of) free school meals (FSM) has played a prominent role, over the years, in defining schools' contexts. There has been a continuing assumption that schools with similar proportions of FSM pupils face similar challenges. An obvious point to make in this respect is that whilst knowing the proportion of pupils on free school meals provides information about the size of the group experiencing some degree of poverty (measured in economic terms), it provides no evidence about the circumstances of the remainder. In one school the remaining pupils might be just about eligible but, for one reason or another, not quite, whilst in a second they might be spread across the social spectrum from those who are almost eligible to those who are considerably advantaged. Degrees of social disadvantage and social advantage are not necessarily mirror images of each other.

There are limited opportunities for schools to influence the proportions of FSM pupils in their care but they have a larger role with respect to determining the perceived extent of some other background factors. The proportions of pupils with 'special educational needs' is one such example. A very small minority of pupils continue to be statemented by their local education authorities – statementing is a device through which more sustained support and resources can be mobilized for a pupil. Meanwhile, the 'special needs' of much larger proportions of pupils in difficulty are assessed by their schools. Furthermore, there may be incentives for schools to assess pupils as being in need, perhaps because their LEAs offer additional resources for such pupils. Two schools which appear to be 'similar' in terms of available statistics, then, may actually differ in underlying respects, the variations between them being masked by the processes through which the indicators are calculated. In short, some traditional indicators of disadvantage probably need to be treated with greater caution. As Thrupp (1999) has observed, the 'challenges', if that is the right word, faced by many schools serving very disadvantaged populations is that they are simply overwhelmed by the depth of problems surrounding them.

Some reinterpretation of other dimensions of 'disadvantage', which have historically been treated as important because they were associated with low levels of pupil performance, may also be required. Ethnicity, for example, can no longer simply be assumed to be a correlate of lower academic progress. Some 'minority' groups now perform notably well and make good progress over time whilst English as a Second or Alternative Language frequently emerges as a positive correlate of pupil progress. Many pupils, who come into their schools hardly speaking English, seem to pick it up fairly quickly, their relatively low starting points providing scope (with greater experience of the English system and their schools' support) for considerable progress to be demonstrated.

There has been a tendency, over the years, to control aspects of disadvantage at the level of the individual pupil. Part of being disadvantaged, however, seems to involve having restricted access to more advantaged peers. More than three decades ago, the Coleman Report (1966) showed that who pupils went to school with mattered as much as the ways in which the schools they attended were resourced. Since that time a range of studies have shown that there is an additional effect on pupil progress from 'group effects' over and above that explained by individual circumstances. A pupil on free school meals, for example, in a school where there is a high proportion of pupils who are also on free school meals, seems to make slightly less progress than a 'similar' pupil on free school meals in another school where lower proportions are in receipt of them. However, the size and consistency of this effect does seem to depend on the other factors being taken into account. It has been more powerful when no controls for prior performance have been available, less obviously so when they have.

Whilst the dominant view of 'context' has related to the social circumstances within which a school finds itself, other structural factors may also need to be taken into account. Historically, schools which have been in a position to select their intakes have secured a competitive 'edge' for their pupils; this edge has applied, to a greater or lesser extent, across the sector. By the same token schools which have not been in this position have had their results correspondingly depressed; again this seems to have been a sector effect. As Goldstein and Woodhouse (2000: 356) have argued, 'the actions and characteristics of any one school are linked to those of other schools'.

Such clear patterns are more difficult to discern in systems which are organized along comprehensive lines. A recent analysis of the effects of competition on schools in six LEAs, however, suggests that those which came low in the local pecking order experienced a depressing effect on their results – they all improved more slowly than others in their localities (Levacic and Woods, 2001). Schools serving disadvantaged communities are, of course, overrepresented in these latter categories.

Outcome measures

The most ubiquitous yardstick currently in use to compare schools' performance is five or more grades A*–C at GCSE. This measure is widely recognized as a comparatively 'high' hurdle and owes its origins to the levels of performance to which, in the past, all/most pupils in grammar schools were expected to aspire. Its relevance to schools in disadvantaged circumstances is more limited. Whilst such schools can reasonably expect to have some pupils for whom such targets are appropriate, the numbers in any one cohort are likely to be relatively small. Furthermore, small changes can lead to apparently dramatic swings in performance. For example, with 100 pupils in a cohort and just 10 per cent getting five or more A*–Cs, no less than a 50 per cent improvement could be secured by moving just five pupils up by a grade in a couple of subjects. Exclusive use of this measure almost certainly guarantees the emergence of an uneven picture with respect to progress.

In recent years other yardsticks of performance have become more widely used. The one or more A*–G passes measure, for example, records any exam success whatsoever and, as such, is a relatively 'low' hurdle. The Exam Points Score, meanwhile, gives credit for all levels of performance and not just the highest grades. The former is, perhaps unfortunately, often dismissed as representing too low a hurdle, even for the most disadvantaged of schools. Certainly, schools in similar circumstances differ in the extent to which they attempt to secure high percentages in relation to it; it is perhaps better treated as a measure of a school's inclusion policies. The advantage of the Exam Points Score, by contrast, is that it gives credit for different approaches to raising performance; all exam grades are taken into account.

A significant weakness of current evaluative efforts is that views of performance tend to be restricted to a single measure. Performance in terms of the 'high' (five or more A*–C) and 'low' (five or more A*–G) hurdles discussed above is certainly correlated but only weakly; it is possible for a school to make progress in terms of one measure without necessarily gaining much in terms of the other. In view of the different strengths and perceptions of the measures outlined above, there could be some advantage to employing all three with comparisons being based on a 'frontier' approach in which all three feature. Further attention might also be given to other measures of school performance such as pupil attitudes, attendance, self-reported truancy and exclusions. Whilst these latter measures are not a substitute for academic performance, they are almost certainly precursors of it.

Searching for trends and progress over time

The major policy concern in 'low performing' schools is, of course, that performance should rise. Actually demonstrating that change has occurred is, however, difficult. Performance seems likely to move both up and down over relatively short time-scales. Strategies for discerning whether there is any overall trend are therefore important.

Two approaches suggest themselves with respect to tracking schools' efforts – the school's own recent history and progress in 'similar' schools. Of the two approaches, comparison with a school's previous history has, perforce, been the more widely used. Clearly the aspiration here has been that the school should improve each year on its previous performance. The problem is that one needs to know something about the extent to which performance has varied in the past. If performance moves up a bit and down a bit on a regular basis, then one may merely be tapping into what is basically 'natural variation'. If the baseline is set in a year when performance has been particularly depressed, upward movement may be no more than a reversion to the 'natural' level or trend; conversely, if it is set after a 'good' year, it may appear that little or no progress has been made in the following year.

The problem can be demonstrated in practical terms by reference to the experiences of a group of schools judged by Her Majesty's Inspectors to have made sufficient 'progress' to come off Special Measures in 1998 (see Table 5.2). The analysis looked for evidence both of improvement and of trends over time.

Table 5.2 indicates that in seven out of the 11 schools there was clear evidence of improvement in terms of performance on the five or more A*–C measure since 1994 (see column 1); the remaining four schools will doubtless have had to convince HMI that they were making progress in terms of other measure(s) of performance not incorporated into the table. Furthermore, when one looks at improvement across all 11 schools from 1995 to 1997, there appears to have been an upward trend. However, notwithstanding the aggregate pattern across the schools, in only one of them (School J) was this trend produced by an annual increase. In short, evidence of aggregate level improvement seems to have resulted from a pretty varied pattern at the level of the individual school.

In the post-Special Measures period, five out of the 11 schools had improved on their 1997 performance by 2001 (see column 3). However, whilst there was evidence of an overall trend across all 11 schools across this period, patterns in individual schools were again mixed – focusing on the aggregate picture can be misleading. Whereas just one of them had managed to sustain a clear trend over the first time-period, none actually managed to do so over the second. Indeed, only three of the schools (G, H and K) improved on both their 1994 and 1997 baselines. Whilst there may be particular (and possibly enduring) problems in schools experiencing Special Measures, such findings should alert us to the difficulties of applying conventional assumptions about the linear nature of improvement efforts to particular schools. It seems pretty common for performance, over the short term, to fall as well as rise. What really matters, of course, is whether there is any evidence of a longer-term and underlying dynamic.

An alternative (but potentially compatible) approach is to set up some kind of 'comparison' group against which to judge performance

Table 5.2: Improvement trajectories of a cohort of secondary schools coming off Special Measures in 1998

School ID	(1) Improvement from 1994 base whilst in Special Measures?	(2) Trend over the years 1995–97 in Special Measures?	(3) Improvement post-1997 after Special Measures?	(4) Trend over the years 1998–2001 since Special Measures?
All 11 schools	Yes	Yes	Yes	Yes
G	Yes	No	Yes	No
B	Yes	No	No	No
C	No	No	No	No
D	No	No	No	No
H	Yes	No	Yes	No
A	No	No	Yes	No
E	No	No	Yes	No
F	Yes	No	No	No
I	Yes	No	No	No
J	Yes	Yes	No	No
K	Yes	No	Yes	No

Source: DfES Performance Tables.

Note: The performance measure employed is five or more A*–C grades.

and progress. A seemingly obvious group to compare such schools with would be similarly low-performing schools, matched in terms of socio-economic and other relevant background factors. But, whilst matching on contextual characteristics (such as poverty and special needs) is better than simply using comparisons with schools at the same overall levels of performance, there is a risk that the most important characteristic of all, namely each school's general level of 'effectiveness' in contributing to its pupils' progress, will be ignored.

A framework for thinking about how to track school improvement over time has been laid out elsewhere (see Gray *et al.*, 1999). This argues that the key dimension for comparison should be 'changes to schools' effectiveness'. In general terms, the argument runs, different strategies may be required to help schools at different levels of 'effectiveness' to improve. A school which is already functioning at a 'high' level of effectiveness is not usefully compared with one which is currently 'low' – the challenges, along with the options available to remedy them, differ in crucial respects.

Some of the alternatives are laid out in Table 5.3. In terms of relevant background or contextual factors, all four schools seem comparable. Whilst any of Schools 2, 3 or 4 might typically feature as comparison schools for School 1, only School 4 shares all the social and educational challenges and starts from a comparable base in terms of its effectiveness.

The struggle for stability and the development of 'capacity'

It is self-evident that for a school to improve it must start to change. But where should the change process commence? In recent years attention has increasingly focused on the importance of 'capacity-building'. As David Hargreaves has suggested: 'A key idea for linking school effectiveness to school improvement is that of capacity for improvement, which is assumed to characterise a school that sustains its effectiveness by successfully managing change in a context of instability and reform' (2001: 488).

In a recent review of 'research on improving and effective schools in socio-economically disadvantaged areas', Muijs (2003) draws attention to some of the 'main elements that have been found to lead to improvement and effectiveness' (see Table 5.4). The list, although rather bald when presented in this format, has a familiar ring to anyone who has been working in this field for much of the last decade.

Clearly, if schools in disadvantaged areas were able to address such factors systematically, then a good deal of benefit would probably result.

Table 5.3: Comparing schools in terms of contextual factors and effectiveness

	School 1	School 2	School 3	School 4
Free School Meals	similar (band)	similar (band)	similar (band)	similar (band)
Special Needs	similar	similar	similar	similar
Other Contextual Factors	similar	similar	similar	similar
'High' Effectiveness	–	–	'high'	–
'Average' Effectiveness	–	'average'	–	–
'Low' Effectiveness	'low'	–	–	'low'

Indeed, if they were to address most of them, then one would probably want to argue that they had developed the 'capacity for improvement'. To quote Hargreaves again: 'An improving school increases its intellectual capital (especially its capacity to create and transfer knowledge) and its social capital (especially its capacity to generate trust and sustain networks) to achieve the intellectual and moral excellences, by learning successfully to use higher leverage strategies based on evidence of 'what works' and/or innovative professional practice' (2001: 489).

Table 5.4 is premised on the assumption that schools which are 'under-performing' need to develop a greater capacity to innovate. They will move forwards, in short, in proportion to their ability to take on and implement ideas and approaches which are, to some degree, new to them. There is another side to schools' improvement efforts, however, which is perhaps rather more routine and humdrum but nonetheless equally important. This perspective suggests that what distinguishes schools that are under-performing from others is, in part, their difficulty in generating sufficient stability to serve as a platform for improvement efforts. In Hargreaves' terms, their opportunities for improvement would be restricted: 'Low social capital, among teachers entails lack of trust and networking among colleagues, who thus fail to share their pedagogic knowledge and skills, derived from research evidence or personal experience' (2001: 488).

Developing sufficient social capital can be especially difficult for schools serving disadvantaged communities. A number of considerations come together to impede change. Table 5.5 lists some of the factors mentioned in a recent review of the experiences of schools 'causing

Table 5.4: Some areas related to the development of 'capacity' in schools serving socio-economically disadvantaged areas

Developing teaching and learning
Involving parents
Becoming learning communities
Emphasizing continuing professional development
Enhancing effective leadership
Creating an information-rich environment
Developing a positive school culture
Making use of external support
Developing resource utilization

Source: Muijs (2003)

concern' which probably contribute to their problems in initiating key changes (Gray, 2000).

In short, a framework for evaluating change which gives equal prominence to the search for stability alongside the development of greater 'capacity' is probably required. In Figure 5.1 the two perspectives are presented together.

In order to create the conditions for sustained improvement schools need to move slowly and by degrees towards the upper right-hand quadrant in Figure 5.1. Unfortunately, we know relatively little about causal sequences in this context but movement from left to right along the 'unstable/stable' continuum may well need to happen before significant vertical movement in relation to capacity development can occur. As Maden (2001) reminds us, what distinguished schools in her study, which were continuing to improve 'against the odds', was their 'fusion of

Table 5.5: Some potential barriers to developing 'capacity' in schools serving socio-economically disadvantaged areas

Context and planning:
Uncertainty about school's future
Under-recruitment, low numbers of pupils on roll
Use of school as 'last resort' for problem pupils excluded from other local schools
Building problems (split sites, temporary accommodation, lack of specialist facilities)
Financial constraints (limited opportunities to redirect resources)
Structural rigidities (forms of organization reflecting outdated priorities)
Staff-related factors:
Rapid/uneven turnover amongst: senior leadership (head, SMT); middle
management (heads of department); classroom teachers
Mix of staff experience (balance of 'old guard'/ 'new blood')
Dependence on supply staff to cover core teaching functions
Low staff morale and limited will to improve
Lack of knowledge about how to improve
Inappropriate staff attributions in relation to 'under-performance'
Restricted use and experience of 'whole-school' strategies
Limited experience of handling innovation
Pupils:
History of continuing and deep-rooted behavioural problems
Extensive pupil mobility in/out of the school

Source: Gray (2000)

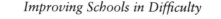

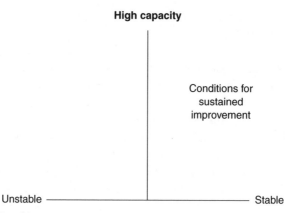

Figure 5.1: Combining perspectives to create improvement

dynamism and calm order'. But which came first? The strategies a school puts in place in the battle for stability are probably at least as important as the skirmishes it undertakes in the name of improvement.

Conclusion

An important shift in the frameworks being employed to judge schools' performance has been taking place in recent years. The trend away from the simplistic approaches that have dominated the public arena needs to be sustained. I began by suggesting that evaluating the efforts of schools in disadvantaged areas has posed a series of problems: performance has tended to be measured against inappropriate yardsticks, sensitivity to difficulties and context has been in relatively short supply and expectations in relation to change and development have often been unduly high. It can be problematic, in such circumstances, to demonstrate that improvement, especially of a more profound kind, has been taking place. From the approaches outlined here, however, I hope it is clear that there are some alternatives.

References

Coleman, J. S., Campbell, E., Hobson, C., McPartland, J., Mood, A., Weinfeld, R. and York, R. (1966) *Equality of Educational Opportunity Survey.* Washington, DC: US Government Printing Office.

Goldstein, H. and Woodhouse, G. (2000) 'School effectiveness research and education policy', *Oxford Review of Education,* 26, 3 and 4, 353–63.

Gray, J. (2000) *Causing Concern But Improving: A Review of Schools' Experiences*, research report. London: Department for Education and Skills.

Gray, J., Hopkins, D., Reynolds, D., Wilcox, B., Farrell, S. and Jesson, D. (1999) *Improving Schools: Performance and Potential*. Buckingham: Open University Press.

Hargreaves, D. H. (2001) 'A capital theory of school improvement', *British Educational Research Journal*, 27, 4, 487–503.

Levacic, R. and Woods, P. (2001) 'Raising school performance in the league tables: disentangling the effects of social disadvantage', *British Educational Research Journal*, 28, 2.

Maden, M. (ed.) (2001) *Success Against the Odds – Five Years On: Revisiting Effective Schools in Disadvantaged Areas*. London: Routledge Falmer.

Muijs, D. (2003) 'Improving and effective schools in disadvantaged areas: a summary of research findings', *Improving Schools*, 6, 1, 5–11.

Thrupp, M. (1999) *Schools Making a Difference: Let's Be Realistic!* Buckingham: Open University Press.

6 Improving Schools in Socio-Economically Disadvantaged Areas: A Review of Research Evidence[1]

Daniel Muijs, Alma Harris, Christopher Chapman, Louise Stoll and Jennifer Russ

CHAPTER OVERVIEW

It is a feature of the field of school improvement and effectiveness that there remains a dearth of substantial literature reviews on schools in difficulty. In this chapter by Daniel Muijs and his colleagues there is an attempt to put that record straight. In reading the chapter it becomes clear that much of the existing rationale for intervention in difficult schools comes primarily from the know-how derived from the effective schools' literature. In the chapter a series of themes are reviewed which characterize contemporary attention – teaching and learning, leadership, data richness, a positive ethos, ambition towards being a learning community, a culture of ongoing professional learning, the involvement of parents, the use of external resources all feature as factors which necessitate attention in challenging schools.

Introduction

The educational reform agenda in many countries reflects a renewed interest in improving schools in difficult or challenging circumstances. Recently researchers have returned their expertise and attention to 'failing' or 'ineffective' schools (e.g., Barth *et al.*, 1999; Leithwood and Steinbach, 2002; Borman *et al.*, 2000; Harris and Chapman, 2001). As Gray (2001: 33) concedes 'we don't really know how much more difficult it is for schools serving disadvantaged communities to improve because much of the improvement research has ignored this dimension – that it is more difficult, however, seems unquestionable'. The reason for this lack of attention resides predominantly in the inherent sensitivity and the complexity of the terrain. Schools that face multiple forms of disadvantage are least likely to be open to critical scrutiny or exposure because they are most often the schools where academic performance is below average.

While it cannot be denied that there is a strong negative correlation between most measures of social disadvantage and school achievement, this is not to suggest that it is impossible to 'buck this trend'. Some schools facing difficult and challenging circumstances are able to add significant value to levels of student achievement and learning (Maden and Hillman, 1996). There is evidence to show that these schools can and do improve levels of student performance and achievement. However, in order to achieve and sustain improvement such schools must exceed what might be termed as 'normal efforts' (Maden, 2001). Recent research has shown that teachers in schools facing challenging circumstances have to work much harder and be more committed than their peers in more favourable socio-economic circumstances. In addition 'they have to maintain that effort in order to sustain improvement as success can be short-lived and fragile in difficult or challenging circumstances' (Whitty, 2002: 109).

Schools located in disadvantaged areas suffer a myriad of socio-economic problems, such as high levels of unemployment, physical and mental health issues, migration of the best qualified young people and, not least, low educational achievement (Gore and Smith, 2001). To compound this, schools in these areas often face other pressures such as challenging pupil behaviour, high levels of staff turnover and a poor physical environment. For these reasons schools in deprived areas have to work harder to improve and stay effective, find it harder to improve and are more likely to suffer steep declines in pupil achievement levels if a successful equilibrium is disturbed; for example, when succession problems occur following retirement of the head (Reynolds *et al.*, 2001)

These specific contextual circumstances suggest that different improvement strategies are required for schools in difficult or challenging circumstances from those in more advantaged circumstances. In this review of the literature we have therefore attempted to look at the evidence concerning school improvement in areas suffering socio-economic deprivation. While research on school improvement in schools in economically deprived areas is still limited, there is clearly a growing consensus around a number of key areas within the field. Many of the strategies found to be effective in schools in economically deprived areas are not exclusive to those schools as they focus, for example, on issues of teaching and learning and collaborative modes of leadership. The order of findings in this review does not reflect a recommended order in which schools should tackle school improvement. Rather, the order reflects the strength of evidence supporting particular approaches to school improvement in this context.

Improving schools in disadvantaged areas

A focus on teaching and learning

A clear focus on a limited number of goals has been identified as a key characteristic of effective and improving schools (Hopkins, 2001; Reynolds *et al.*, 2001). An academic orientation has long been identified as a vital component of effective schools in the UK (Reynolds *et al.*, 2001), and studies in other countries that have looked specifically at schools in areas of high deprivation report similar findings. There are many examples of this in extant research. Connell (1996) studying schools that had moved off the list of poorly performing schools in New York found that the common denominator for all of them was a focus on students' academic achievement, and that all had developed new instructional strategies. Teddlie and Stringfield (1993) likewise found that in ineffective schools in Louisiana the heads focused less on core instructional policies than in effective schools, while a study of 12 effective schools in low-income areas in Quebec found that these schools had a particularly strong focus on core instructional policies. (Henchey, 2001). A strong academic focus was also found in a study of high performing schools in poor areas of Texas (Lein *et al.*, 1996). In Herman's (1999) review of reform programmes in the USA, a strong instructional focus was common to all the most effective programmes. Other researchers have likewise stressed that a focus on teaching and learning is crucial, something which can be encouraged by training staff in specific teaching methods at the start of the school's improvement effort (Hopkins, 2001; Joyce *et al.*, 1999). It is teaching and learning issues that directly influence attainment and learning but research shows that different strategies are used in schools in low Socio-Economic Status (SES) areas (Muijs and Reynolds, 2000).

Research findings show that low SES students need more structure, more positive reinforcement from the teacher and to receive the curriculum in smaller packages followed by rapid feedback (Brophy, 1996). They will generally need more instruction and be more responsive to external rewards (Teddlie and Stringfield, 1993). High levels of structure and clarity were also found to characterize effective schools serving low SES and high ethnic minority populations in one Dutch study (Ledoux and Overmaat, 2001). While mid- and high-ability students do not benefit from praise unrelated to the task, there is some evidence that low achievers do benefit from non-contingent praise, because of the low self-esteem of many of the students (Brophy, 1992). Pupils from lower SES backgrounds have been found to benefit from a more integrated curriculum across grades and subjects (Connell, 1996). Connecting learning to real-life experience and stressing practical applications have been found particularly important to low SES pupils, as has making the curriculum relevant to their daily lives. This may diminish disaffection as well as promoting learning (Guthrie *et al.*, 1989; Henchey, 2001; Hopkins and Reynolds, 2002; Montgomery *et al.*, 1993). According to Mortimore *et al.* (1991) effective teaching in this type of school should be teacher-led and practically focused, but not low level or undemanding. Creating consistency in teaching approach is important for pupils from low SES backgrounds, and has been found to be related to improved outcomes (Connell, 1996).

In their study of schools in high and low SES areas, Teddlie and Stringfield (1993) found that in effective low SES schools there was more emphasis on basic skills and less on extending the curriculum than in effective high SES schools. Likewise, a survey of 366 high-performing schools in high poverty areas found that they had focused more strongly on maths and English by extending teaching time and changing the curriculum so there was a stronger emphasis on basic skills (Barth *et al.*, 1999). A Dutch study found that in effective schools with high numbers of underperforming ethnic minority students there was a strong emphasis on basic skills, and a strongly structured curriculum (Ledoux and Overmaat, 2001). However, other authors claim that pupils from low SES backgrounds are more capable of higher-order thinking than is often supposed and should be exposed to a curriculum that is as rich as that of their advantaged counterparts, built around powerful ideas and focusing on metagcognitive skills (Guthrie *et al.*, 1989; Leithwood and Steinbach, 2002). Interestingly, one school improvement project that chose to narrow the curriculum by aligning it to a basic skills test used by the region (the Iowa Test of Basic skills) failed to show improved performance after two years (Philips, 1996).

Further evidence comes from an American project in which the curriculum of a highly selective private school was transplanted to two high poverty schools in Baltimore (with a large amount of professional development and support through a school-based coordinator). It lead to strong improvements in achievement in both schools, as well as improvements in attendance (McHugh and Stringfield, 1998). A danger with focusing on basic skills in schools with a low SES intake is that by offering them an impoverished curriculum, social divides could be exacerbated rather than diminished. A study of 26 high achieving impoverished schools in Texas showed that both direct instruction and constructivist teaching strategies were employed in these schools, neither seeming inherently more effective (Lein *et al.*, 1996). A similar finding was reported by Ledoux and Overmaat (2001) in their Dutch study; effective schools using a mix of traditional and constructivist methods. Interestingly, in two well-executed studies in the USA and UK, improving schools were found to have emphasized arts (Connell, 1996; Maden, 2001).

While a focus on teaching and learning is crucial, this does, of course, mean that the conditions must be in place in which effective teaching can occur. Maden and Hillman (1996) found that improving schools had all put clear discipline procedures in place and were focused on creating an orderly environment. In particular in disadvantages areas it is crucial to have effective discipline in place. However, this does not mean that schools should be excessively disciplinarian. Valuing pupils and making them feel part of the school 'family' are characteristics of effective schools as is pupil involvement is setting up the rules (Connell, 1996; Lein *et al.*, 1996).

Leadership

It is well-known that leadership plays a key role in school improvement and school effectiveness. The evidence from the international literature demonstrates that effective leaders exercise an indirect but powerful influence on the effectiveness of the school and on the achievement of students in most countries (Harris and Muijs, 2002), an exception being the Netherlands (Ledoux and Overmaat, 2001; Van De Grift, 1990), although there is some evidence that leadership might be increasing in importance there as well (Scheerens, 1998)). In a major review, Hallinger and Heck (1998) report that principals have an indirect, but highly measurable effect on pupils' achievement, explaining up to a quarter of the school level variance in pupil achievement. What form that leadership should take is less clear. Maden and Hillman (1996) did not find one particular leadership style in their improving schools in disadvantaged circumstances, but noted that in many there was shared decision making and collegiality.

Traditionally, leadership has been seen as the preserve of 'great men', inspirational heads who can 'turn round' schools (Harris and Chapman, 2001). Recently, however, there has been a move towards a realization that the most effective means for true improvement lies in more distributed and democratic forms of leadership, involving teachers in leading their schools. The heroic view of leadership has only on occasion been found to be the factor that has led to school improvement (Connell, 1996), while teacher leadership has been found to benefit improvement in a range of studies (Harris and Muijs, 2002). School improvement programmes that have attempted to increase teacher involvement in decision-making report positive effects (IESP, 2001), and heads of improving effective inner-city schools frequently mentioned this as an important approach (in Seeley *et al.*'s (1990) study, for example). Piontek and colleagues (1998) found decentralized leadership, using small teams that made decisions on different aspects, to be typical of improving schools in their study of six high poverty urban elementary schools. In Louis and Miles (1990) study of urban high schools, heads were found to be strongly instrumental in formulating a clear vision for the school and in monitoring performance, but likewise involved teachers and middle managers in school leadership. Involving teachers in developing or choosing a school improvement strategy has been found to be a crucial factor in sustaining improvement in a number of studies.

In Ross and colleagues' (2001) review of the Memphis Restructuring Initiative, it was found that both leadership of the head and teacher involvement were crucial to the success of the programme, the head being more influential on the speed that schools took to implement the reform programme, but teacher commitment being crucial to the quality of implementation. Some experts advocate stronger involvement than is usual of community members as well, involving them in a democratic structure focused on inquiry and school improvement (Joyce *et al.*, 1999; IESP, 2001). They suggest setting up a body specifically charged with school improvement, composed of management, teachers, local business leaders and members of the community. In Maden and Hillman's (1996) study, however, effective schools in disadvantaged areas differed in their extent of community involvement.

Open communication is obviously an important aspect of this collaborative, distributive leadership style, and has been demonstrated to characterize improving and effective schools in a number of studies (Harris and Chapman, 2001; Hughes, 1995). Collaboration and trust have likewise been found to be related to effectiveness in schools in difficult circumstances, and are crucial to being able to deal with the emotional disruption change almost invariably causes (Lein *et al.*, 1996; Stoll, 1999). Leadership in improving schools is often described as transformational, seeking to satisfy higher needs and engaging the full person of the follower, as opposed to transactional leadership, which is characterized by exchange relationships (Harris and Chapman, 2001; Reynolds *et al.*, 2001). Transformational leadership is seen as better able to cope with complex situations (such as schools in economically deprived areas), and was, along with instructional leadership (focus on teaching and learning) found to be a characteristic of effective leaders in Hallinger and Heck's (1998) review.

Leadership in effective and improving schools has also often been described as instructional, which means that effective heads focus on teaching and learning issues more than on other (administrative) aspects (Connell, 1996; Stoll, 1999; Teddlie and Stringfield, 1993). This also means being cognizant of current teaching and learning theories, and/or helping and encouraging staff to continually develop their expertise in these areas. Leaders must also be seen by staff to be learners themselves (Stoll, 2001).

Creating an information-rich environment

Data richness has long been found to be an important component of effective and improving schools in studies in the UK, the USA and Canada: Reynolds and colleagues' (forthcoming) study of HRS components, for example, finding this factor to be strongly related to improvement. Being data rich means that data can be turned into information used as a basis for school and classroom decision-making (Henchey, 2001; Hopkins, 2001; Joyce *et al.*, 1999; Reynolds *et al.*, 2001). Data-rich schools collect and centralize a wide variety of data, including exam results, standardized and teacher-made test results, questionnaires and qualitative data, but this is of no use if it is not used to improve schooling.

Data-rich schools continuously interrogate existing test data to see whether initiatives are working, or whether there are problems with achievement in particular areas or with particular populations, and have been described as 'inquiry minded' (Barth *et al.*, 1999; Earl and Lee, 1998). Schools can also decide to collect the views of pupils and/or teachers in a particular area through the use of questionnaires on student and staff satisfaction, school conditions and even teaching methods (Etheridge *et al.*, 1994). Data have been successfully employed in looking at the effectiveness of new programmes, teaching styles or mentoring methods (Connell, 1996). Data on factors such as attendance may likewise be useful, as can disaggregating data according to such factors as gender and ethnicity. Target setting, which should always be based on data in order for it to be realistic and useful, has likewise been found to be a spur to school improvement in many schools (Reynolds, 1996).

Creating a positive school culture

School culture is one of the most widely cited elements in both improving and effective schools, but also one of the most problematic. Some cultural elements that are amenable to intervention and that can aid school improvement have been identified. Joyce *et al.* (1999) suggest that a blame-free culture is essential if the conflict that renewal efforts can cause is to be alleviated. Open communication and supportive leadership can help achieve this.

Coherence is a key element to improving schools in economically deprived areas. Pupils need to know what to expect, and have the right to experience a high quality of teaching in all lessons. Continuity in approach is important, especially for pupils from disadvantaged areas, and this should be extended to coherent assessment methods across subjects and interrelated courses within the school curriculum (Hopkins and Reynolds, 2002; Leithwood and Steinbach, 2002). Maden and Hillman (1996) found a coherent approach to be common to all the effective schools they studied, with the school development plan often lying at the heart of this approach.

High expectations are consistently cited as being important to pupil achievement, and this is likely to be the case to an even stronger extent in schools serving a low SES population (Lein *et al.*, 1996; Montgomery *et al.*, 1993). Producing high expectations is, however, more easily said than done, be it among teachers, pupils or members of the community. Producing success stories can help teachers divest themselves of negative beliefs about pupils, as can the setting (and achieving) of ambitious targets for pupil achievement in the school. High expectations need to be transmitted to pupils. This can be facilitated through monitoring of pupil work, positive feedback, and the setting of demanding but realistic pupil targets (Maden and Hillman, 1996).

A shared vision has often been cited as an important element of the culture of effective schools, though in Reynolds and colleagues' (forthcoming) analysis of the relationship between components of the High Reliability Schools model and improvement in achievement (5 per cent A–Cs) between 94 and 01, no relationship was found between having a shared vision and improvement.

One problem for schools in economically deprived areas is high staff turnover, which can disrupt the school. In one study for example, it was found that schools with similar demographic characteristics that were differentially effective differed in terms of staff turnover, the less effective schools experiencing higher turnover rates (Hughes, 1995). The causality here is unclear, however, as low turnover could be both a cause and a result of higher effectiveness. Obviously, levels of turnover can strongly affect school culture, with stable staff having a positive effect in that a shared culture and vision can be maintained, but, in some cases, also leading to complacency and a resistance to change.

School improvement efforts have also been found to be strongly influenced by teachers' beliefs in the effectiveness of the intervention, which influences their work rate and enthusiasm. In Borman and colleagues' (2000) study, teacher beliefs in these areas were found in part to be subjective, but mostly to be influenced by objective factors, and therefore by evidence of prior success of the improvement plans or project and by the effect it was seen to have in their school and on their pupils.

Becoming a learning community

An increasing body of research has pointed to the need for schools to become learning communities, engaged in continuous improvement efforts and enquiring into both within school conditions and out-of-school developments, rather than being merely reactive to inspection or government initiatives. Such schools are open to change and experiment, and engaged in continuous improvement through enquiry into existing practices and evidence-based adoption of innovation (Joyce *et al.*, 1999). In professional learning communities the teachers in a school and its administrators continuously seek and share learning and then act on what they learn. The goal of their actions is to enhance their effectiveness as professionals so that students benefit. Learning schools are characterized by the presence of reflective dialogue, in which staff conduct conversations about students and teaching and learning, identifying related issues and problems (Louis and Kruse, 1995; Louis and Miles, 1990). This emphasis on creating learning communities differs from approaches to school improvement that have focused on elements such as target setting, targeting pupils at the c/d borderline, support for behaviour management and mentoring by adults, which tend to be focused on specific strategies which may well work in the short term but will not create the conditions for continuous improvement (Hopkins, 2001). There is some evidence that becoming a learning community is linked to student outcomes, one review pointing to increased meaning and understanding of taught content by pupils as well as teaching being more adapted to student needs (Hord, 1997).

Stoll (1999) sees continuous learning as dependent on the school's capacity, which is in turn influenced by the school's teachers, the school's social and cultural learning context and the school's external context. The 'teacher as learner' is central to school capacity, teachers' practices being the key to school improvement and school effectiveness. Teachers are, however, not working in isolation, but are influenced by their inter-actions with others, their pupils, the school culture, its management, etc. Finally, the external context (community, policy, global culture) of the school influences the school's capacity. Louis and Kruse (1995) identified supportive leadership from the head, with a strong element of distributed leadership, as a crucial factor in creating learning communities, along with a shared vision focused on student learning, respect and trust among colleagues and, not least, the existence of physical spaces were staff could meet to engage in reflective dialogue.

One problem with school-based improvement efforts can be that much time is expended on inventing solutions that already exist or that are inferior to existing solutions. That is why it is important for schools to study the existing knowledge base, or connect to external agencies (such as local education authorities or higher education institutes) and to pilot new ideas on a small scale before stringently analysing them (Joyce *et al.*, 1999; Piontek *et al.*, 1998). Learning organizations are by definition not overly conservative, however. Experimentation is encouraged and different approaches are tried out and appraised for effectiveness. An example of this was found in a large-scale study of schools in economically deprived parts of Texas, where high-performing schools were found to experiment with new approaches, but did so in a careful way, attempting always to select approaches that were likely to lead to improved student outcomes and monitoring success (Lein *et al.*, 1996).

Joyce and colleagues (1999) suggest the building of small teams that engage in school improvement activities, which will increase teachers' sense of belonging and minimize alienation. Teamwork is crucial to creating a learning community. Hughes (1995) found teamwork, along with strong teacher accountability, to be a factor that differentiated more from less effective schools in West Virginia, while in their study of improving high poverty schools in Massachusetts, Piontek and colleagues (1998) likewise found that teamwork and positive communication were present in all these schools. These teams will need to be fluid, impermanent and oriented to achieving a particular goal (Lein *et al.*, 1996). To be effective, collaboration needs to be purposeful and action-focused. Working together on a shared plan of action, for example, is likely to lead to positive outcomes and avoids the pitfalls of 'contrived collegiality' (Connell, 1996)

Schools need to ensure that time for common lesson planning and collective enquiry is available – for example by rescheduling the school timetable – and that teachers can observe one another's lessons, as many instances of good practice will be found in any given school (Connell, 1996; Guthrie *et al.*, 1989; Seeley *et al.*, 1990). In a learning community, staff will talk with each other about teaching and learning, creating an inquisitive and change-oriented environment, in which one innovation leads to another, as found in Piontek and colleagues' (1998) study of improving high poverty elementary schools. Another way to help create learning communities in schools is to focus on the departmental as well as the school level, which because of its greater proximity to the pupil, as well as to the fact that in the large secondary school it is usually the forum within which teacher practice and discussion are actually framed, can have a greater effect on improvement and can be a practical way to start to create learning communities within the school (Harris, 2001).

Continuous professional development

Research shows that improving schools spend more time and effort on professional development that stable schools (Freeman, 1997). Many effective and improving schools therefore have policies in place that support staff professional development (Henchey, 2001; Reynolds *et al.*, 2001), and a strong continuing professional development element is common to the most effective school reform programmes in the USA (Barth *et al.*, 1999; Herman, 1999). Staff development was found to be one of the most important factors in Reynolds and colleagues' (forthcoming) analysis of the relationship between components of the High Reliability Schools improvement programme and improvement in participating schools over a five-year period.

Professional development does not just need to be present, however. To be effective, professional development needs to be linked to school and not just individual goals, and needs to be embedded in the workplace (Joyce *et al.*, 1999).

As well as these factors, Joyce and Showers (1995) suggest that the following elements should be present in effective staff development:

1 Practical, classroom-relevant information. Teachers prefer training to be grounded in practical classroom concerns.
2 An element of theory aimed at fostering deep understanding.
3 The incorporation of some element of demonstration, which likewise increases the effectiveness of training substantively.
4 A combination of these three makes an even bigger difference: their combination makes more difference than one would expect from just adding the individual effect of these components.
5 Coaching and feedback, through the use of mentor programmes for example, makes even more difference, leading to further large positive effects on student outcomes.

In most cases, professional development in schools at present does not include all these elements and, where it does, there is not a sufficient amount of time allocated for teachers to attain mastery in the area studied (Joyce *et al.*, 1999). Time needs to be made for professional development; for example, by reserving all staff meetings for professional development, as done in at least one of the improving schools studied by Piontek and colleagues (1998).

Involving Parents

Joyce and colleagues (1999) have stated that for true school improvement to occur, schools must become communities, involving parents and local businesses as well as teachers and heads, while in their interviews with principals of effective inner-city schools Seeley and colleagues (1990) found that heads frequently mentioned parental involvement as crucial to school improvement. In another US study of improving schools in economically deprived areas, the most successful school was found to have a very strong community outreach programme, including links with local businesses and parents (Borman *et al.*, 2000). In Barth and colleagues' (1999) survey study, effective schools were found to specifically involve parents in raising standards through improving their knowledge of the curriculum and capacity to help their offspring, rather than use them largely as fundraisers. In their UK study Maden and Hillman (1996) found that effective and improving schools attempted to involve parents, but often found this very hard to achieve, while Connell (1996) in his study of improving schools in inner-city New York found that parents were involved in some schools but by no means all, with Henchey (2001) reporting similar findings in Quebec. While this study suggests mixed results, a large-scale study in Louisiana actually found that effective low SES schools discouraged parental involvement in order to keep at bay negative home influences, while effective high SES schools did have strong parental involvement programmes (Teddlie and Stringfield, 1993). In another US study, it was found that in order to optimize effectiveness, school leadership teams needed to hear and take account of parent (and student) voices, but paradoxically that having parents on the team was detrimental to professional relations (Chrispeels *et al.*, 2000). Coleman (1998) widens the discussion by seeing parental involvement as part of a triangular relationship between teachers, parents and students, each able to reinforce positive attitudes in the other. Parents and students both need to participate fully in the school. Teachers who were able to improve student commitment and attitudes were characterized by positive attitudes towards parents. However, achieving parental involvement is one of the most difficult areas of school improvement in economically deprived areas.

One large-scale study found that children in low SES homes were subject to only half as much parental talk as children in high SES families, with talk aimed at them more likely to be negative than in high SES families, all of which led to a widening vocabulary gap that meant that by age 3 high SES children had a vocabulary three times as great as those in low SES households (Hart and Risley, 1995). Family education programmes and integrated school and social services have therefore been suggested as necessary in this type of environment, and have been found to have positive effects (Leithwood and Steinbach, 2002; Montgomery *et al.*, 1993; Mortimore, 1991). School community workers – members of the community who liaise between school and home, monitor families' health and welfare needs and give parents information on school programmes and helping their child learn – have been employed success-fully in some effective school districts, as has helping parents with limited English proficiency by providing English language classes (Borman *et al.*, 2000). Some schools have successfully improved parental involvement by supplying them with incentives to come to school, such as providing them with transport, childcare or, in one highly impoverished district, laundry facilities (Guthrie *et al.*, 1989; Leithwood and Steinbach, 2002). It is also important to note in this respect that Maden and Hillman (1996) found that it was easier to get parents involved at the nursery stage of their children's education than later on in their schooling.

External support

External support is another factor that has been found to be important to school improvement in disadvantaged areas (Reynolds, *et al.*, 2001). One way of generating external support is through the creation of networks of schools that can support one another, by providing leadership at many levels, supplying social and technical support, sharing and generating of ideas, disseminating good practice, providing a different perspective and creating larger professional learning communities (Hopkins and Reynolds, 2002) – a strategy taken on in the UK for example through the learning schools network.

Another form of external intervention can be external monitoring. In Freeman's (1997) study in Louisiana, improving schools were found to be subject to more district monitoring of school improvement that stable schools. One form of external monitoring are school inspections, such as those done by Ofsted, which have a clear school improvement remit. However, recent research has shown claims that inspections lead to school improvement to be somewhat dubious. Chapman (2002) conducted ten case studies of schools facing challenging circumstances, finding that the closer staff were to the classroom the more negative they were about the inspection process. He also found that Ofsted inspections led to a more autocratic leadership style and more 'short-termist' leadership. Where respondents reported improvement following inspection most claimed these changes could have been made without Ofsted. Respondents were more positive about HMI inspections. On the other hand, external pressure can clearly set school improvement processes in motion in some cases, and a mix of external pressure and support has been found to be a catalyst for change (Fullan, 1991). However, accountability and improvement are not the same thing, and attempting to combine the two in one process will inevitably cause tensions and contradictions (Earley, 1998).

Local Education Agencies have also often been seen as providing support for school improvement by acting as a resource for professional development, helping schools with data analysis and giving intensive early support to schools (Watling *et al.*, 1998), a role that would correspond with the facilitative rather than commanding role seen as useful for LEAs in Seeley's (1990) principal interviews.

Resources

If school improvement is to succeed, proper resourcing has been shown to be essential (Reynolds *et al.*, 2001). A direct link between the success of school reform initiatives and the amount of funding school received was shown in at least one study (Borman *et al.*, 2000), while strong financial support (from the Annenberg Foundation) is undoubtedly one reason for the success of school improvement initiatives in New York and Chicago (IESP, 2001). Lack of resources following cuts was found to be the most common reason for school reform programmes to fail in Nesselrodt and colleagues' (1997) study of the implementation of school improvement strategies in the USA.

Just providing resources is unlikely to automatically lead to improvement, however. In some studies, effective schools have been found to be more effective at deploying resources, acting as 'wise consumers' (Piontek *et al.*, 1998) and to be more proactive at finding resources (Connell, 1996).

A further problem can be that providing resources to ineffective schools may itself be an ineffective strategy as these schools do not have the management and leadership capacities to use these extra resources in a way that is likely to lead to improvement. This means that management capacity may have to improve before resources are put into failing schools.

Finally, it is important to note that changes in a school's composition can influence rates of school improvement (Thrupp, 1999). This is not only a result of the long-established link between school achievement and social background, but also because context effects whereby an increasing number of pupils from higher SES backgrounds in school intakes can create a change in a school culture once a certain 'critical mass' has been reached (Van der Velden and Bosker, 1991).

Sustaining improvement

While many schools can make short-term improvements, sustaining improvement is a big challenge, particularly for schools in economically deprived areas. However, the amount of research on this issue is very limited. One study that has looked at sustaining school improvement has been undertaken by Maden (2001). This study visited schools that had managed to sustain improvement over time even though they were in difficult or challenging circumstances. Their findings pointed towards the importance of changes in the wider context. Changes in the local economy and school intake were important. Some schools had experienced 'gentrification', leading to a more middle-class intake, while in other areas the situation had declined. In all cases, this influenced sustainability of improvement.

Staff changes were also found to be a key element in altering the effectiveness of the school. Recruiting high-quality teachers was therefore an important strategy in schools where staff changed substantially. Staff stability was also a factor as many of the schools had not changed staff over a five-year period (ibid.). Other important factors included shared values that were clearly articulated, involving other adults, targeting, coaching and mentoring, and an academic focus. Sustained improvement was related to schools with 'value-added curricula', with after-school programmes, study skills centres and a strong ICT component. Again, no one leadership style was found to be present. It was notable that schools where improvement was sustained had strong external networks and connections and tended to interpret national initiatives rather than be run by them (ibid.).

American studies have come to similar conclusions. Datnow and Stringfield (2000) report the following factors to be instrumental in sustaining school improvement:

1 Teachers see methods as effective.
2 Heads manage and support change.
3 There is a culture of continuous professional development.
4 Active recruitment of high-quality staff.

Looking at long-term effective schools in poor areas, Stringfield and Herman (1998) identified factors very similar to those mentioned as part of school improvement in poor areas, such clear goals and data richness, but also a valuing of reliability over efficiency or low costs. This study also pointed to the importance of ongoing monitoring of success.

Florian (2000) studied state reform efforts in four state districts implemented ten years earlier to see whether reform had been sustained. The following factors were found to influence whether this had been the case:

1 Schools becoming learning organizations, with an ongoing disposition to learning.
2 New practices integrated into school routine.
3 District policies that support reform.
4 Creating a structure in which professional development and collaboration are to the fore.
5 Leadership that maintains a consistent vision.
6 Consistency between school and district level policies and good relations between the two.
7 A supportive political context.

Commentary

It remains the case that schools located in contexts of multiple disadvantage have levels of performance that, in most cases, fall short of national averages. This not only presents them with a range of practical difficulties but also asks a great deal of those who lead the school to 'buck' this particular trend. There is little doubt that it would be simpler to pass off responsibility to other sectors or to governments and claim there is little schools can do. As Stoll and Myers (1998) note there are no 'quick fixes' for schools facing challenging circumstances but there is an emerging evidence base to suggest that there are certain strategies schools can adopt that are successful. In summary, these include a focus on teaching and learning, effective distributed leadership, creating an information-rich environment, creating a positive school culture, creating a learning environment and a strong emphasis on continuous professional development. These have all consistently been demonstrated to be important in improving schools in difficult or challenging circumstances. We undoubtedly need to know much more about improving schools in difficult circumstances and particularly how such schools sustain improvement over time. Increasingly, the evidence base is pointing towards the possibilities and potential of learning communities in building the capacity for school improvement. This offers a powerful way of generating opportunities for teachers to work together.

As the long-term patterning of educational inequality looks set to remain, leaders in schools facing challenging circumstances must look for strategies and approaches that might assist their school, in their context, with their students. The strategies outlined in this chapter offer schools in disadvantaged or difficult circumstances and those who research in this area some guidance about enhancing improvement potential. While the limitations of the research base are acknowledged, the degree of consensus concerning the key elements of improving schools in disadvantaged areas are worth serious consideration.

Note

1 This chapter is based on an article published in the journal *School Effectiveness and School Improvement*.

References

Barth, P., Haycock, K., Jackson, H., Mora, K., Ruiz, P., Robinson, S. and Wilkins, A. (1999) *Dispelling the Myth. High Poverty Schools Exceeding Expectations*. Washington, DC: The Education Trust.

Borman, G. D., Rachuba, L., Datnow, A., Alberg, M., Maciver, M. and Stringfield, S. (2000) *Four Models of School Improvement. Successes and Challenges in Reforming Low-Performing, High Poverty Title 1 Schools*. Baltimore: Johns Hopkins University, Center for Research into the Education of Students Placed At Risk.

Brophy, J. (1996) *Teaching Problem Students*. New York: Guildford.

Chapman, C. (2002) *OFSTED and School Improvement: Teachers' Perceptions of the Inspection Process in Schools Facing Challenging Circumstances*. Coventry: University of Warwick Institute of Education.

Chrispeels, J. H., Castillo, S. and Brown, J. (2000) 'School leadership teams: A process model of team development', *School Effectiveness and School Improvement*, 11, 1, 20–56.

Coleman, P. (1998) *Parent, Student and Teacher Collaboration: The Power of Three*. Thousand Oaks, CA: Corwin Press.

Connell, N. (1996) *Getting off the List: School Improvement in New York City*. New York: New York City Educational Priorities Panel.

Datnow, A. and Stringfield, S. (2000) 'Working together for reliable school reform', *Journal of Education for Students Placed At Risk*, 4, 1, 125–61.

Earl, L. and Lee, L. (1998) *Evaluation of the Manitoba School Improvement Program*. Toronto: Walter and Duncan Gordon Foundation.

Earley, P. (ed.) (1998) *School Improvement After Inspection?* London: Paul Chapman Publishing.

Etheridge, G. W., Butler, E. D. and Scipio, J. E. (1994) 'Design of a learning community for urban learners: the Memphis plan'. Paper presented at the Annual Meeting of the American Educational Research Association, New Orleans, LA, 4–9 April.

Florian, J. (2000) *Sustaining Educational Reform: Influential Factors*. Aurora, CO: Mid-Continent Research for Education and Learning.

Freeman, J. A. (1997) 'Contextual contrasts between improving and stable elementary schools in Louisiana'. Paper presented at the Annual Conference of the Mid-South Educational Research Association.

Fullan, M. (1991) *The New Meaning of Educational Change*. London: Cassell.

Gore, T. and Smith, N. (2001) *Patterns of Educational Attainment in the British Coalfields*. Sheffield: DfES.

Gray, J. (2000) *Causing Concern but Improving: A Review of Schools' Experiences*. London: DfES.

Guthrie, L. F., Guthrie, G. P., Van Heusden, S. and Burns, R. (1989) *Principles of Successful Chapter 1 Programs*. San Francisco: Far West Laboratory for Educational Research and Development.

Hallinger, P. and Heck, R. H. (1998) 'Exploring the principal's contribution to school effectiveness: 1980–1995'. *School Effectiveness and School Improvement*, 9, 2, 157–91.

Harris, A. (2001) 'Department improvement and school improvement: a misssing link?', *British Journal of Educational Research*, 27, 4, 477–86.

Harris, A. and Chapman, C. (2001) *Leadership in Schools Facing Challenging Circumstances*. London: DfES.

Harris, A. and Muijs, D. (2002) *Teacher Leadership: A Review of Research*. Coventry and London: University of Warwick Institute of Education – General Teaching Council.

Hart, B. and Risley, T. R. (1995) *Meaningful Differences in the Everyday Experience of Young American Children*. Baltimore: Paul Brookes.

Henchey, N. (2001) *Schools That Make A Difference: Final Report. Twelve Canadian Secondary Schools in Low-Income Settings*. Kelowna, BC: Society for the Advancement of Excellence in Education.

Herman, R. E. (1999). *An Educator's Guide to Schoolwide Reform*. Washington, DC: American Institutes for Research.

Hopkins, D. (2001) *Meeting the Challenge. An Improvement Guide for Schools Facing Challenging Circumstances*. London: DfES.

Hopkins, D. and Reynolds, D. (2002) *The Past, Present and Future of School Improvement*.

Hord, S. M. (1997) *Professional Learning Communities: Communities of Continuous Inquiry and Improvement*. Austin, TX: Southwest Educational Development Laboratory.

Hughes, M. F. (1995) *Achieving Despite Adversity. Why Some Schools Are Successful in Spite Off the Obstacles They Face. A Study of the Characteristics of Effective and Less Effective Elementary Schools in West Virginia Using Qualitative and Quantitative Methods*. Charleston, WV: West Virginia Education Fund.

Joyce, B., Calhoun, E. and Hopkins, D. (1999) *The New Structure of School Improvement*. Buckingham: Open University Press.

Joyce, B. and Showers, B. (1995) *Student Achievement Through Staff Development*. New York: Longman.

Ledoux, G. and Overmaat, M. (2001) *Op Zoek Naar Succes. Een onderzoek naar Basisscholen die Meer en Minder Succesvol Zijn voor Autochtone en Allochtone Leerlingen uit Achterstandsgroepen*. Amsterdam: SCO-Kohnstamm Instituut.

Lein, L., Johnson, J. F. and Ragland, M. (1996) *Successful Texas Schoolwide Programs: Research Study Results*. Austin, TX: The University of Texas at Uastin, The Charles A. Dana Center.

Leithwood, K. and Steinbach, R. (2002) *Successful Leadership for Especially Challenging Schools*.

Louis, K. S. and Kruse, S. D. (1995) *Professionalism and Community: Perspectives on Reforming Urban Schools*. Thousand Oaks, CA: Corwin Press.

Louis, K. S. and Miles, M. B. (1990) *Improving the Urban High School: What Works and Why*. New York: Teachers College Press.

Maden, M. (ed.) (2001) *Success Against the Odds: Five Years On*. London: Routledge.

Maden, M. and Hillman, J. (eds) (1996) *Success Against the Odds: Effective Schools in Disadvantaged Areas*. London: Routledge.

McHugh, B. and Stringfield, S. (1998) *Implementing A Highly Specific Curricular, Instructional and Organisational High School Design in a High Poverty Urban Elementary School: Three Year Results*. Baltimore: Johns Hopkins University, Centre for Research on the Education of Students Placed At Risk.

Montgomery, A., Rossi, R., Legters, N., McDill, E., McPartland, J. and Stringfield, S. (1993) *Educational Reforms and Students Placed At*

Risk: A Review of the Current State of the Art. Washington, DC: US Department of Education, OERI.

Mortimore, P. (1991) 'Bucking the trends: promoting successful urban education'. Paper presented at the Times Educational Supplement Greenwich Annual Lecture, London.

Muijs, R. D. and Reynolds, D. (2000) *Effective Mathematics Teaching: Year 2 of a Research Project.* Paper presented at the International Conference on School Effectiveness and School Improvement, Hong Kong, 8 January 2000.

Nesselrodt, P., Schaffer, E. and Stringfield, S. (1997). 'An examination of the disruption of special strategies programs', in S. Stringfield *et al.* (eds) *Special Strategies Studies Final Report.* Washington, DC: US Department of Education.

Philips, J. (1996) 'Culture, community and schooling in Delta County: state assistance and school change in schools that would never change'. Paper presented at the Annual Meeting of the American Educational Research Association, Montreal, Quebec.

Piontek, M. E., Dwyer, M. C., Seager, A. and Orsburn, C. (1998) *Capacity for Reform: Lessons fron High Poverty Urban Elementary Schools.* Portsmouth, NH: RMC Research Corporation.

IESP (2001) *Final Report of the Evaluation of the New York Networks for School Renewal 1996–2001.* New York: Steinhardt School of Education, Institute for Education and Social Policy.

Reynolds, D. (1996) 'Turning around ineffective schools: some evidence and speculations', in J. Gray, D. Reynolds, C. Fitz-Gibbon and D. Jesson (eds) *Merging Traditions: The Future of Research on School Effectiveness and School Improvement.* London: Cassell.

Reynolds, D. (1998) 'The study and remediation of ineffective schools: some further reflections', in L. Stoll and K. Myers (eds), *No Quick Fixes: Perspectives on Schools in Difficulties.* London: Falmer Press.

Reynolds, D., Hopkins, D., Potter, D. and Chapman, C. (2001) *School Improvement for Schools Facing Challenging Circumstances: A Review of Research and Practice.* London: DfES.

Reynolds, D., Stringfield, S. and Muijs, D. (forthcoming) *Results from the High Reliability Schools Project.*

Ross, S. M., Sanders, W. L., Wright, S. P., Wang, L. W. and Alberg, M. (2001) 'Two and three year achievement results from the Memphis restructuring initiative', *School Effectiveness and School Improvement,* 123, 323–47.

Scheerens, J. (1998) *De Bevordering van Schooleffectiviteit in het*

Basisonderwijs. 'S Gravenhage: Ministerie van OC7W, Directie Primair Onderwijs.

Seeley, D. S., Niemeyer, J. S. and Greenspan, R. (1990) *Principals Speak: Improving Inner-City Elementary Schools. Report on Interviews with 25 New York City Principals.* New York: City University of New York.

Stoll, L. (1999) 'Realising our potential: understanding and developing capacity for lasting improvement', *School Effectiveness and School Improvement,* 10, 4, 503–32.

Stoll, L. (2001) *Enhancing Internal Capacity: Leadership for Learning.* NCSL. Retrieved 13/08/2002, from http://www.ncsl.org.uk

Stoll, L. and Myers, K. (1998) *No Quick Fixes: perspectives on schools in difficulty.* London: Falmer Press.

Stringfield, S. and Herman, R. (1998) 'Research on Effective Instruction for At Risk Students: Implications for the St. Louis Public Schools'. *Journal of Negro Education,* 66, 3, 258–88.

Teddlie, C. and Stringfield, S. (1993) *School Matters: Lessons Learned from a 10-Year Study of School Effects.* New York: Teachers College Press.

Thrupp, M. (1999) *Schools Making a Difference: Let's be Realistic! School Mix, School Effectiveness and the Social Limits of Reform.* Buckingham: Open University Press.

Van De Grift, W. (1990) 'Educational leadership and academic achievment in secondary education', *School Effectiveness and School Improvement,* 1, 1, 26–40.

Van der Velden, R. and Bosker, R. (1991) 'Individuen, Gezinnen an Buurten: Sociale Determinanten van het Onderwijsniveau', *Mens en Maatschappij,* 66, 3, 277–325.

Watling, R., Hopkins, D., Harris, A. and Beresford, J. (1998) 'Between the devil and the deep blue sea? Implications for school and LEA development', in L. Stoll and K. Myers (eds) *No Quick Fixes. Perspectives on Schools in Difficulties.* London: Falmer Press.

Whitty, G. (2002) *Making Sense of Education Polity.* London: Paul Chapman.

Part Two
Improving the Process of Schools in Difficulty

7 Putting Our Heads Together: A Study of Headteacher Collaboration as a Strategy for School Improvement[1]

Mel Ainscow, Mel West and Maria Nicolaidou

CHAPTER OVERVIEW

Strategically, our focus of attention with schools in difficulty is on the single organization. It is a procedural fact that for the most part, a team of people will worry around a school that is defined as being in special measures. In this chapter, Mel Ainscow, Mel West and Maria Nicolaidou report on an intervention in one school where just such an approach was adopted, but what was characteristically different in this case was the way that the team was drawn from the LEA and three headteachers from relatively successful local schools. The authors argue that in some situations school-to-school cooperation offers the possibility of educational improvement for schools facing difficulties. It also highlights the observation that the learning is mutual within a relationship where people external to school come to the support of those inside. It is an important message, suggesting that schools in difficulty are not going to have the internal capacity to solve their problems alone, even when new headteachers and senior leaders are appointed, so systems of support which enable experienced colleagues from elsewhere within the locality to engage with colleagues in schools in difficulty are a vital feature of the systemic development of intervention but not without their own associated difficulties.

The fact of the matter is that organisations such as schools ... will, like dragons, eat hero-innovators for breakfast.

(Georgiades and Phillimore, 1975)

This chapter provides an account of the events in an urban secondary school that serves one of the country's most economically deprived areas. The school was fifteenth from the bottom of the national GCSE league table when former Education Secretary David Blunkett announced a crackdown on poor examination results in March 2000. All schools where less than 15 per cent of pupils achieved five A*–C grades in GCSEs for three consecutive years would be given a 'Fresh Start'; that is, they would be closed and reopened with a new name, new management and new staff.

At this particular school, the relevant figure that year was just seven per cent.

In fact, the school did not close. Instead, three relatively successful schools in the same LEA partnered it in order to foster improvements in the school's work. Cooperation between the headteachers of the four schools was the central strategy used. The LEA provided support for the initiative and some additional funding was provided by the Standards and Effectiveness Unit at the DfES.

Subsequently, an HMI inspection report said that there had been a significant change in the school's ethos, with both teaching and behaviour improving significantly. Then in the summer of 2002, when the annual GCSE results were published, BBC television reported that the school had recorded a 400 per cent rise in its 'top grades' and that truancy rates had been halved, making it 'among the most improved schools in Britain'.

The story raises some interesting possibilities with respect to ways of supporting schools in difficult circumstance, although the approach adopted is not without its own difficulties. In this chapter we provide an evaluative account of what happened in order to draw out the strategic implications of the experience. Our analysis concludes that school-to-school cooperation offers greater possibilities for school improvement than existing strategies that rely solely on the efforts of individual headteachers who are expected to act as 'hero-innovators'. At the same time, we argue that considerable care needs to be taken in introducing such approaches more widely.

Schools causing concern

The government has made various attempts to improve schools that are seen to be a cause for concern. One such approach was 'Fresh Start'. Modelled on ideas imported from the USA, this approach placed particular emphasis on the role of the headteacher as the key, leading to the use in the media of the term 'superhead'.

The particular US scheme on which Fresh Start is based is known as 'school reconstitution', and had already fallen into some disrepute in the USA at the same time as it was being introduced into England (Hardy, 1999). The underlying idea was to jump-start dysfunctional schools, many of them in poor urban areas, by bringing in a fresh, new committed staff.

There is little definitive research on whether reconstitution actually improves student achievement, though early reports on San Francisco's first four reconstituted schools were positive. Yet even proponents of reconstitution concede that it can be a wrenching process and can take years to yield positive results. Rozmus (1998) states that if it is done superficially, or with little thought to the kinds of programmes that will be implemented, reconstitution can lead to even further problems in the future. Orfield (1996) writes: 'Reconstitution is major surgery, drastic intervention, it's like trying to rebuild a rapidly deteriorating train as you're running down the tracks.'

The same author points to three attributes observed in those schools that appear to have benefited from this approach in the USA: each featured dynamic leadership from the principal (i.e., headteacher); in each case the principal had deliberately nurtured a collaborative relationship with the school's teachers; it was also noted that the schools had been given additional resources in the form of funding, new programmes and professional development. Results in the reconstituted schools, however, have been especially disappointing in recent years (Miner, 1998). It seems that whilst some reconstituted schools show marked improvement, others appear to be mired in the same, or worse, difficulties as before reconstitution (Hardy, 1999). Even Orfield, who was prominent in the San Francisco experiment, now recognizes the limits of reconstitution. He suggests that it is like open-heart surgery, necessary in some cases but very costly and needs a very strong supporting team to give it a reasonable chance of success. It is not a strategy that could be used on any scale, he argues, since it requires considerable investment in order to create a new school in situations that are, by their nature, inherently difficult (Orfield, 2000).

Nevertheless, in England Fresh Start was presented as 'an option' for local education authorities to use in tackling school failure. Blackstone (2000) argued that it offered a 'radical approach to securing school improvement for failing schools showing insufficient evidence of recovery'. The scheme, under which the worst performing schools, as identified by Ofsted, were re-launched under a new name, a new headteacher, without the staff who were unsuccessful in reapplying for their old jobs, and with extra cash, has, however, been dogged by controversy, including the resignation of the first four 'superheads' to be appointed.

These headteachers, handpicked on the basis of previous success, were appointed to provide the charismatic and dynamic leadership deemed necessary. It became one of the most visible examples of how the government hoped that struggling schools could be turned around. The act of closure was not only symbolic but also allowed a 'clear-out' of pupils and teachers, and corresponding changes in parental perceptions, as well as the injection of significant new resources. However, the costs of such interventions were high, up to £1 million in capital works and half that again for restructuring on top of the regular budget. Furthermore, it was unlikely to achieve immediate results, since starting points were low and the culture of deprivation and underachievement was so deeply embedded in the communities served by the schools. Thus, even if the initiative was to make a difference, it would inevitably take time to show.

With the benefit of hindsight, what went wrong can be traced to a mix of immediate and underlying problems. Once 'superheads' were appointed, they were confronted by three sets of problems: the pupils, the staff and the fabric of the school. These headteachers came into post at a time when the government was attempting to force down the exclusion rate nationally and make it into an unacceptable option. Under intense media focus, it became difficult, therefore, to remove 'trouble-makers' quickly and effectively as they dealt with inherited discipline problems.

Staffing was another common problem. New, inspirational teachers were seen as being essential in a Fresh Start school, but local bureaucracy, arguments with teacher unions, employment tribunals, problems with differential pay and contracts made staff hard to recruit and retain, particularly at senior management levels. In practice, none of the Fresh Start schools opened with a complete senior management team in place.

Despite these many obstacles, some of the schools did make progress. What the successful ones have found, however, is that high profile strategies have limited leverage for moving practice forward. Rather, what seems to be needed are strategies based on firm principles, a united staff and governing body, sound policies and strong support for classroom learning.

Collecting evidence

Our evaluation of this particular school-to-school initiative was, therefore, set in the context of the apparent disappointment of these attempts to give schools a 'fresh start'. It was carried out over a period of a year, during which our aim was to capture the story of what was happening, drawing on the different views and experiences of many of those involved, and to analyse this body of evidence in order to draw out possible lessons that could be of value to policy-makers and practitioners.

The following methods were used to collect evidence:

- **Document analysis**   A range of documents provided by the participating headteachers was analysed. This analysis provided the basis for writing an overall history of the initiative. From this it was possible to create a short 'timeline' of key events that could be used by members of the evaluation team to carry out focused interviews, as recommended by Ainscow *et al.* (1995)

- **Meetings** A number of meetings were held with the four head-teachers involved. Typically these were about two hours long and were used to establish contexts for what had been done within the partnership and to discuss about what had been learnt as a result of the activities that occurred over the period.

- **Shadowing** Through a series of shadow observation visits we were able to get close to key informants and, indeed, to record detailed accounts of their practice. Visits were usually followed by immediate de-briefing sessions during which they could offer their reflections and the researcher would also share impressions.

- **Interviews** Impressions gained through observation and shadow visits were compared with other data gained through more systematic forms of interview. In order to introduce an element of triangulation, interviews were carried out separately from shadow visits and by different members of the research team.

All the available evidence was carefully analysed as the basis of an account that is summarized in this chapter. In constructing this account, we tried as much as possible to respect the different views we heard. In the main these differences focus on matters of detail, as people with varied perspectives tell of their experiences. At the same time, they remind us of the social complexity involved.

Getting started

There were approximately 450 students on roll, although the school was originally intended for 1,000. As we have explained, it serves one of the most deprived areas in the country and had examination results that might have warranted a Fresh Start. However, an alternative solution was suggested by the headteacher of another local high school. His initial proposal was that he should be placed in charge of both schools. However, since the existing head of the school in difficulty was due to retire, the LEA had already advertised for a successor. In the event, the idea of having a team of headteachers was agreed. This suggestion was much more acceptable to the governing body, the members of which were committed to the employment of a headteacher for their school.

The actual mix of expertise provided by the consultant heads proved to be very important. In particular, one had a strong track record in relation to finances and resources; another had a reputation for target setting and putting in place strategies enabling students to work towards individual learning targets; and the third had expertise in marketing and working with unions. As we will explain, when the story unfolded it became clear that these were exactly the sorts of issues that outsiders could address, leaving those within the school to concentrate on leadership and capacity-building.

By the time of the interviews for a new headteacher in April 2000, the basis for the partnership arrangement was largely in place. Nevertheless, the successful candidate was given the choice as to whether or not she actually wanted to work with the proposed consultancy team. In that sense, therefore, the decision to go ahead was ultimately *hers*.

This trio worked largely 'in the background' between April and September 2000, at which point the new headteacher took up her duties. During this period, schemes and systems were devised, division of responsibilities between the team members were discussed, and decisions were made about procedures and protocols. The headteachers all maintain that in these ways they set in place an infrastructure that would allow them to operate in the knowledge that they had the security to deal with unanticipated difficulties. For example, they set in place a protocol about working with the media, and conduit arrangements through which all media inquiries were to be fed.

From Easter to the end of the summer term 2000, the three heads worked with the headteacher-elect to produce a 'comprehensive plan for raising achievement'. They also agreed that their roles would mainly be as consultants, each contributing the equivalent of one day a week of support and advice. From the outset it was noted that the new head and the school's governing body would always 'have the last word'. This meant that as she talked with her new colleagues, it was absolutely clear to them that she was 'in charge' of the school. One of the consultant heads explained that sometimes they encouraged her to 'undermine them' in a mild sort of way and to always make her own decisions. He commented, 'Hers had to be the heroic kind of model; she had to be everywhere, and we did some of the things that time didn't allow her to do, I suppose.'

In practice, one of the consultants dealt with financial issues; another took on the task of analysing the pupils' results and developing appropriate forms of target setting in order to improve achievement; and the third dealt with the overall arrangements for the initiative, including issues to do with the 'marketing of the school' in the local district. One of the consultants explained that in taking on these tasks the three heads 'freed [the new head] from a lot of the background nitty-gritty stuff that would distract her from being upfront'. Consequently she was able to concentrate on day-to-day management issues, not least the urgent matter of creating a more supportive climate for learning in the school.

The work of the consultant heads

Once the project was announced to the staff there were some signs of mistrust and resentment towards what was proposed and how it was going to be put in place. The fact that some of the staff had to take early retirement or re-apply for their own jobs caused particular turbulence, and some of the teachers remember the period as being a 'confusing and stressing time'.

Apparently, the proposed redundancies overshadowed the events surrounding the retirement of the existing headteacher. One member of staff explained:

> Everyone realized that his days were gone and that there was a new game in town, the only game in town, and everyone had to stand full square behind that. And people's minds were made up then. And some staff, made the decision that yes, this was what we were going to do.

Some staff stated that they could be supportive of the in-coming head because they felt that the changes that she and the consulting heads were proposing made sense, especially those related to the curriculum. At the same time, others recall having doubts and uncertainties about what was being proposed.

This period of mixed reactions presented the three consultant heads with a series of dilemmas and sensitive situations, as they explored ways of developing their new roles. Initially the retiring head was still in position and this made it difficult for them to collect further information and intervene directly. They were also conscious that some of the staff might react negatively to their presence in the school, since there were understandable loyalties to the retiring headteacher.

Once the heads did begin visiting the school, however, they became increasingly concerned about what they found. For example one of them explained:

> The shock was that the finances were in a very poor state and the school was vastly overstaffed. In fact, it was uneconomic. The staff had a perception that it was all OK ... They had dug themselves little holes and jumped in with tin hats on. They had low expectations not only of themselves but also of the students and it didn't take us long to find that out. We didn't find anything that was unexpected other than some comments like, 'what do you expect from children like these'.

The team asked staff to tell them what was wrong. Recalling some of the responses, one of the visiting heads commented:

> We felt that the more we talked to them, the more we actually got the truth. There were lots of things: staff living in the past; others saying, plod on with your head down and get paid; some saying, staff do very little; others feeling neglected, saying they had received no training. They had a middle school mentality: lack of leadership; staff too friendly and relaxed; no monitoring; frustration and a feeling that it was not going anywhere, therefore they felt it wasn't worthwhile. There was a culture of underachievement. There was no culture of children working after school; a lack of determination; no vision; lack of challenge; no rigour, no will, no cooperation, no consistency and no back-up from senior staff.

One head remembered how, during a staff meeting, the three consultants presented their views on a series of overhead projector slides. This including an analysis of the school's targets for improvement: what had been achieved and what might have been achieved. He recalled that some members of staff were clearly shocked. He also said that he 'went through *their* perceptions of the place, which also shocked and somehow angered them. The point was that it was in fact their perception of what went on.'

Referring to the same staff meeting, one of the other consultant Heads said that this was probably the most significant moment in the whole initiative. The consultant head who made the presentation explained:

> I took all the value added data for the LEA and I put a table up which showed the 21 high schools (it hadn't any names on it) and it went from best to worse and I asked where they thought they were as a school. And they all thought they were in the middle or, possibly, even to the left of the middle. And, when I told them they were significantly twenty-first out of 21, they were absolutely shocked. They wouldn't believe it. But the previous Ofsted report hadn't done them any favours because it seemed to be saying that they were doing the best but kids didn't want to go to school. It [the Ofsted report] concentrated on the challenging circumstances without actually looking at the challenges. That was a very interesting moment. Once I had done that ... at that point I think they were prepared to move on.

Remembering this same period one of the teachers at the school commented:

> It was strange. It was like living after Vietnam, when the Americans re-wrote history. Sometimes, listening to what people say about what happened in the past, it was like it was all bad and now all good. It's not the reality of the situation. But the message they had to give that things had to

change was in contrast to what was going on. The past wasn't good, and what is happening now is. And sometimes it's like 1984, trying to get your mind sorted as to what is the actual real past and what is now the official version of the past.

A new headteacher

Once the new headteacher was appointed she took every available opportunity to let the staff know that she was, to use her own words, 'the person in charge ... It was my school and not the other three heads.' Recalling that period, one senior member of staff commented:

> She showed a lot of drive and determination to make things happen. She wanted the kids bringing in equipment in school. Basically, running the school like her place, like a normal school. No one was arguing about that.

Another teacher remembered that she was:

> very impressed with her [the new head's] vision ... And so were most people at the time, we were desperate for that kind of change, and it was very good that she was appointed because we saw her as someone who might take the school forward.

Other staff reported that they had been eager for change because of the difficulties the school had been facing over recent years. The previous headteacher had been popular, 'a safe pair of hands', who had previously been deputy head there for some time, but now some staff wanted 'someone else to come in and show them a new direction'. One long-serving teacher commented:

> The school needed someone to come in and do different things and approach things from a different way.

On the other hand, the announcement in autumn 2000 that there was to be a programme of staff redundancies had a marked impact on staff morale. Many staff remembered this as a very difficult time, particularly for those colleagues who had been at the school for many years. Some staff had to re-apply for and be interviewed for their own jobs.

During the early part of the 2000–01 school year the consultant heads carried out observations around the school and interviewed members of the staff, asking their perceptions of their school. However, some staff recalled that they did not have a personal interview with the new head, as they had been promised. Some felt that this was something that was overlooked. Others were unconvinced by the way in which they were interviewed, arguing, as one person put it, that they felt that they were all 'tarred with the same brush'. Another teacher commented:

> Things were happening so fast that snap decisions were made, about people and faculties, which were not quite accurate. There wasn't much investigation going on. In the interviews questions were asked and people naively said things which perhaps led to their downfall in the end, because a lot of staff left. People opened up and said things that in the end perhaps were used against them in some ways. People though it was a time to get everything off your chest and people did, and I think in the end it was thrown back at people. ... We never knew where we stood with value-added and how far behind other schools we were at the time. And it came as a shock to us. And I don't think the three heads had realized until then that we'd never been party to a lot of the information that senior management had about the position we were actually in with regards to where we actually stood comparable with other schools in similar situations.

In telling the story, the headteacher of the school focused mainly on her own activities, with only occasional mention of the work of the three consultants. Specifically, she felt that they made a major contribution in helping her to restructure the staffing. She also referred to the fact that there was a phase when things were really difficult and when one of the heads would ring her at the end of school each evening. She recalled that this form of personal support was, for her, particularly significant. At the same time, she was firm in her view that 'turning the school round' could not have been done without her presence and leadership from within.

Her account says much about her personal management strategy. In particular, she remembers being struck initially by the low expectations that were there in the school. For example, she noticed that very few of the children brought bags to school in which they could carry books and equipment. She decided that she must insist that every student had a bag. She recalled what happened:

> So, I did this sort of big speech of how it all starts from here. You know, head up, shoulders back, in we go. And I just said, you've all got to bring bags and if you haven't got a bag tomorrow you will be sent to my office. If they hadn't got a bag, I gave them an Aldi carrier bag. I said, I want you to give that back tomorrow. And bingo, by the end of the first week every child had a bag.

She recalls that many of the teachers said it would not be possible to implement such a requirement, but she persisted and the strategy was successful. She saw this as being a key factor in getting students to do their homework, since without bags there was little transfer of books between home and school.

Similarly, she persisted in implementing policies about the completion of homework, the wearing of school uniform, lunchtime arrangements and the raising of school attendance rates. In the case of this latter policy, she established a team of people who would chase up students who were not attending.

She also recalls having to address some equally difficult issues regarding the work of some of the staff. For her, the budget crisis that the school faced on her appointment provided opportunities for encouraging some staff to take early retirements and for others to move on to posts elsewhere. She also believes that one or two senior members of staff left because they could see the pressure they were going to experience as procedures were tightened and efforts focused.

Patrolling the school

One example of the new head's leadership style could be seen in the introduction of 'school patrols'. The senior management team of four developed a model of working whereby each of them patrolled the school, going in and out of every classroom a number of times during each day. The head also encouraged all of them to follow a similar style of intervention that she modelled, a style that is insistent on certain kinds of behaviour and attitude.

Shadowing the head on these patrols is an interesting experience. She walks directly into every classroom and, without being invited to do so, speaks across the teacher, addressing students and, at the same time, addressing the member of staff as well. She explains that she is conscious of the danger of appearing to undermine her colleagues and this is clearly a potential danger. On the other hand she believes that the way she does this appears to avoid this trap.

Often, during a classroom visit, she will speak to an individual student who she is 'checking on'. Where students are reported to her by a teacher as misbehaving, or not doing their work appropriately, she then talks directly to them. For example, in one classroom, in a rather exaggerated tone of voice, she addressed one of the students, saying: 'I'm very disappointed with you, Darren, and I want you to apologize to Miss. She comes here to teach and she certainly does not have to tolerate such behaviour.' In these situations her manner is both supportive of her colleagues and, at the same time, critical of certain student's actions, many of whom are clearly intimidated by the experience.

At times she can appear to be quite aggressive with individual students, particularly those who are found to be standing outside the room, having been sent out of class by a teacher. Similarly, students seen to be misbehaving between lessons or not getting to their next class quickly, may be withdrawn and given the task of collecting litter around the school. In ways such as these, it seemed that the head and her senior team appear to take personal responsibility for inappropriate behaviour. They also use similar strategies for celebrating the efforts and achievements of students

In discussing this style of 'management by walking about', the head explained that it is extremely demanding of her time and, indeed, the time of her senior colleagues. It also means that she takes on a lot of the discipline issues that arise within the school. Nevertheless, it appeared to have been a highly successful strategy for supporting staff and, indeed, transforming the overall climate within the school. The head summed this up:

> The kids expect me to be in evidence. And my leadership team do the same. And that's why it's a very well disciplined school now. You walk around now and what you will see is an extraordinary level of kids on time for lessons.

Subsequently, the head took the decision to reduce the use of this strategy in order that she could have what she describes as 'a more balanced set of relationships' with the students in the school.

Determining the impact

During this time, considerable changes were made in the curriculum, particularly at Year 10 where new GNVQ programmes were introduced. Cooperation between the partner schools gradually involved other groups of staff, not least in order to address difficulties in certain subject areas. Attention was also given to the improvement of the physical environment, through decoration and displays, and there were further plans for improving those parts of the school that were rather unpleasant.

Two years into the work of the partnership. HMI argued that there was evidence of a 'massive change' in the school's ethos, with teaching and behaviour, in particular, improving significantly. The proportion of pupils gaining five higher GCSEs rose to 10 per cent in 2001, truancy levels had been halved and the proportion of pupils gaining five or more A–G grades improved by 20 percentage points to 94 per cent. Then, in the summer of 2003, more striking improvements were announced, with 33 per cent of students achieving at least five grade A*–C at GCSE.

The head herself feels that the partnership arrangement has been beneficial when advertising for new members of staff, particularly in a context where people tend to be reluctant to take the risk of moving to schools that are in difficulty. For example:

> We actually interviewed somebody who was a front-runner for the secondary science post in the summer and he said at the end of the interview, 'If this project all falls apart this school could close, couldn't it?' We said 'Yes, but it won't!'

The three consultant heads argue that the whole experience has been a steep learning curve for them too and, indeed, for all the staff that have been involved. They also point out that the project involved an element of risk taking, since if it had failed 'the consultant heads had quite a lot to lose, as well as the school'.

As things turned out, the three heads all feel that their involvement has benefited them and their schools. For example, one of them, having been in post for many years, during which time his school has become very successful, is convinced that it has helped him to 'think again' about his own practices. He describes, too, how discussions with his colleague heads have led him to reflect on different leadership styles.

The same head emphasized the importance of the trust that existed between the three consultants. He reflected that the experience had not been threatening to them since they had a shared goal and shared responsibility: they all wanted the school to succeed. Consequently, they were able to work collaboratively:

> But the real beauty is that we don't threaten one another; there is no competition between us. It's collaborative all the time.

He was also convinced that the power of the strategy came about as a result of this collaborative emphasis between a group of practising heads:

> The consultant head model can work because it takes some of your time but not all of it, and because we work as a team ... and no matter what you do, money, resources, policy, you can only get schools out of difficulty through positive leadership. I'm convinced of that.

Similar comments about the benefits about being involved were echoed by the other two consultant heads. One said:

> The development allowed me to continue with my present job, but also to take new directions without giving up everything that I've built and everything I've got. So it's almost risk-free career development for me, in that I can go off in a new direction but still remain the same in some respects. So

it seemed to me a perfect opportunity and I also got to work with two other people that I knew very well and respect.

Another agreed:

The biggest personal gain was to see two other experienced heads work at an operational and a strategic level, because you don't normally see that.

He found this process intellectually challenging, stimulating and eye opening:

I've learnt things … particularly about political manipulation, that I would never even have dreamt of … and I've also seen somebody who has an in-depth understanding of curriculum and student performance that has really opened my eyes to what's possible.

He stressed that because of the nature of the project they had had to be consistent and fully engaged:

It was not something we could leave on the shelf and revisit in or three months time. It was about commitment and involvement; it was real and immediate.

Doubts were expressed by the consultants about whether the model could be replicated with an existing headteacher remaining in post, 'unless they were uniquely humble'. They agreed that changing the headteacher is probably a necessary first step in addressing the problems in schools facing difficulties. Commenting on what might happen if they were invited to do this type of project with a serving headteacher in place, one of the consultants said:

I think it would be much more difficult because they would be on the defensive, quite naturally, unless they were extremely focused and extremely realistic about the situation they were in, and open and receptive to receiving help. Otherwise, I can't see how this model would work. Because if you had a resistant head it would be next to impossible to do the kind of things we've done.

Making sense of the experience

It seems, then, that school-to-school cooperation *can* be an effective strategy for supporting schools facing difficulties and, indeed, for induction to headship in difficult circumstances. Having said that, we are anxious to stress that it does not present a simple, straightforward recipe that can be lifted and easily replicated in other contexts. Indeed, our concern is that any publicity that arises from the publication of this account could lead to naive beliefs that it represents a panacea for addressing educational difficulties.

In drawing lessons, therefore, we aspire to provide a commentary that will be useful to others who are interested in moving practice forward in contexts facing similar challenges. However, in doing so we are keen to respect the complexity of what has occurred and, indeed, the limitations of our own investigations.

As we have shown, this particular initiative has involved a complex mix of social processes that has clearly had a significant impact on attitudes, relationships, practices and learning outcomes for staff and students alike. It is impossible to say which of the many ingredients has been most significant. This being the case, it seems sensible to assume that it is through the interaction of the different elements that the power of the approach is achieved.

In attempting to make sense of the experience, we draw particular attention to three inter-connected strands of activity that would need to be considered by those wishing to adopt a similar approach elsewhere. These strands are: preparing the ground; getting together the correct mix of expertise; and ensuring trust.

It is clear that the lead-in period was both significant and messy. The period was also rich in events that had the potential to create tensions and even conflict, both in the school and in the wider context. The leadership provided by one of the consultant headteachers, who clearly had considerable status and credibility in the district, and his cooperation with senior staff in the LEA were, therefore, essential elements in setting up appropriate arrangements for taking the initiative forward.

Beyond leadership and cooperation, however, there was also a need for considerable skills of diplomacy in negotiating with governors (in the four schools) and in reassuring members of staff, who were understandably disturbed by what must have seemed baffling circumstances and unprecedented proposals. Here, loyalties towards the previous regime and policies, and fears about personal career uncertainties, added to the sense of turbulence that existed. And, of course, during the planning phase of the project those coming in from outside had to deal with the continued presence of the retiring head, who from all accounts was well respected and admired.

Those who set up the partnership arrangements were, to a large degree, successful in dealing with all these potential difficulties. Consequently, important tasks were carried out prior to the arrival of the newly appointed headteacher, including the formulation of a plan of action based on sound evidence as to the situation on the ground. The availability of such a plan enabled her to 'hit the ground running', to an extent that would have been impossible under normal conditions. As a result, she knew what she had to do and she set about her tasks immediately on her arrival in the school.

The decision to involve a team of headteacher consultants and, therefore a group of schools, proved to be an essential factor in the success of the partnership. All the schools were known to be performing well and, perhaps even more significant, all three consultant heads were recognized as successful school leaders. But, perhaps even more important, was the range and types of expertise that together they brought to the situation. In essence they were able to share responsibility for those tasks that have the potential to occupy the time and energy of any newly appointed head, thus leaving her relatively free to concentrate on those day-to-day issues that can only be addressed by those who are always available in the school.

As we saw, the areas on which the consultant heads concentrated included: external relations and marketing, budgets and resources, staffing, and target setting. Time was also saved in addressing these areas because, unlike the newly appointed head, the three consultants had close knowledge of local arrangements, organizations and people. Meanwhile, the head and her senior team were able to focus most of their energy on the key areas of building supportive relationships and raising expectations. This was achieved by ensuring that they had a much higher level of presence around the school and in the classrooms than is usually the case when new heads and management teams take up their duties.

Their strategies for raising expectations focused on three groups. First of all, the interventions of the management team encouraged a greater sense of self-esteem amongst *the students*. New policies were introduced, such as those to do with attendance, behaviour and homework, and then, most significantly, persistent and insistent measures were taken to ensure that these policies were consistently implemented throughout the school.

Second, considerable efforts were made to raise expectations amongst *the staff*. In particular, attention was given to ensuring that all staff members felt that they always had support available as they dealt with difficulties in their lessons and around the school. And, where necessary, in-service training was provided to support them in responding to new requirements. All of this was carried out within what can only be described as an 'upbeat' atmosphere, where success was constantly recognized and celebrated. Finally, the headteacher paid attention to convincing *the local community* that the school was changing and to convincing parents that it could achieve good results for their children.

Whilst having an appropriate range of expertise was a necessary condition for the success of the partnership, in itself it was insufficient. Also needed were attitudes and relationships within which all this expertise could be used in an effective way. It is here that the potential for difficulty becomes so obvious.

First of all, there is the potential for difficulties created by factors at the macro policy level. In particular, within a context in which national educational policies are based on the principles of parental choice and competition between schools, what are the incentives for headteachers to offer one another help and support? And, within such a context, how can arrangements be made that will allow open and trusting working patterns to be established?

Then, at the micro level, there is a relative minefield of potential difficulties when a team of established and successful headteachers appear to have super-ordinate status over a newly appointed and inexperienced head. This relationship also had a gender dimension, with three established male heads supporting a novice female head. The evidence is that those involved managed to avoid these possible difficulties, and their approach is worthy of close scrutiny by those in other contexts that are seeking to follow a similar trail. Once again here, we stress that the account does not provide a recipe but, rather, a basis for reviewing necessary ingredients.

An important factor was the strong and open relationships that existed between the three consultant heads, who knew each other prior to the initiative. They then spent considerable time in helping one another to clarify their roles, including the need to define the boundaries of their activities. In addition, protocols were devised that meant that each partner was certain as to what was to be expected and how difficulties would be addressed.

The establishment of clarity about roles, responsibilities and responses between the three consultants was, then, the basis of agreements with the new head. Perhaps as a result, she was able to define her own boundaries of activity in respect to what the outsiders would be seeking to contribute. And, as we have seen, she was very firm and determined in confirming to everybody involved that it was 'her school' and that it was her responsibility to 'turn it round'.

Implications

Informed by our evaluation, we offer a series of questions that would, we argue, need to be addressed by those involved in attempting to use school-to-school support as a strategy for helping organizations that are in difficulty. We stress that the answers to these questions are likely to be particular to each context and that they must take account of local circumstances and available resources.

The questions are as follows:

1 Preparing the ground
- Are all key stakeholders in agreement with the introduction of the strategy?
- Is there clarity about the purposes amongst these stakeholders?
- Are those organizations and individuals that are to be involved in providing support recognized as being successful in their own working contexts?

2 Getting together the correct mix of expertise
- Do those who are to be involved in providing support have the range of expertise and experience that is needed?
- Is the headteacher of the school that is the focus of support able to establish confidence and authority amongst staff, students, parents and governors?

3 Ensuring trust
- Is there clarity about boundaries, such that those involved have no doubts about their roles and responsibilities?
- Are there agreed protocols as to what actions will be taken in the light of difficulties?

Having drawn out this agenda we feel that it is also important to remind readers about the limitations of our study, some of which suggest certain reservations that need to be kept in mind. We are aware that, despite the care that we have taken to check the accuracy of our evidence, we can only provide a partial account of everything that has happened. There are also issues arising from the relatively short timescale of our investigations. So, for example, whilst we have pointed to evidence of striking progress in three years or so, we cannot give any informed judgement as to the potential for longer-term growth.

Here, of course, as with all forms of school improvement, the issue of sustainability remains a challenge. In this respect there are a number of factors that are rather particular to the context we have described. First of all, the school is in an environment where families have a choice of schools within easy distance. This being the case, there remains the worry that however much progress the school makes in respect to the quality of education it provides, other local schools with stronger reputations will continue to be the preferred choice. If so, the school will inevitably experience a range of constraints that will set limits on how much further improvement can be achieved, particularly in respect to the improvement of aggregate test and examination scores.

Second, there are uncertainties as to the capacity of the existing arrangements to support longer-term improvement efforts. In particular, we do not know whether the fact that outsiders have taken responsibility for a range of key strategic issues has allowed those within the school to develop their own expertise in addressing these areas. Could it be, for example, that allowing a new headteacher to concentrate most of her efforts on certain tasks means that she has missed out on other professional learning opportunities that are normally part of the early years in post?

In these respects, further discussion needs to take place as to what forms of longer-term support is needed. This leads us to think that those who are planning similar initiatives should design longer-term strategies than those that have been developed in this particular case. Furthermore, such strategies need to have a more detailed plan for the disengagement of the support that is to be provided by partners from other schools.

Final thoughts

The evidence of this study suggests that, under certain conditions, school-to-school cooperation offers a promising strategy for bringing about educational improvements in contexts that are facing difficulties. Indeed, it can be argued that it points towards a possible new direction for school improvement policy and practice more generally. It also shows that the practical involvement of experienced colleagues in the development of a newly appointed headteacher offers important strategies for growth to all parties. Not the least interesting of our findings is the extent to which the experienced heads felt they too had grown through the experience.

Since 1988 the educational reform agenda has included a strong rhetoric of increased autonomy for individual schools. This was based on the argument that previous approaches used by LEAs had led to a sense of dependence that had failed to deliver the required improvement in educational quality. It is now becoming increasingly clear that an approach that relies solely on individual schools developing their own improvement strategies is, similarly, not able to bring about widespread progress, particularly in the context of economically poor urban contexts. It seems, then, that we may be witnessing the emergence of a 'third way', that of school-to-school inter-dependence (Ainscow and Tweddle, 2003).

Such an orientation assumes that school improvement does have to be led from 'the inside', building on the expertise and energies that exist, but that added value can be provided through cooperation with those in neighbouring organizations. It is a way of working that can contribute to improvements in all participating schools, whatever their current stage of development. However, it would seem to have particular relevance in contexts that are a cause for concern.

Note

1 An earlier version of this chapter was presented as a paper at the International Congress for School Effectiveness and Improvement in Sydney, Australia, January 2003.

References

Ainscow, M., Hargreaves, D.H. and Hopkins, D. (1995) 'Mapping the process of change in schools: the development of six new research techniques', *Evaluation and Research in Education*, 9, 2, 75–89.

Ainscow, M. and Tweddle, D. (2003) 'Understanding the changing role of English local education authorities in promoting inclusion', in J. Allan (ed.) *Inclusion, Participation and Democracy: What is the Purpose?* London: Kluwer Academic Publishers, pp. 165–77.

Blackstone, B. (2000) 'Fresh Start Schools', *Hansard*, 18 May.

Georgiades, N.J. and Phillimore, L. (1975) 'The myth of the hero-innovator and alternative strategies for organisational change', in C. Kiernan and F. P. Woodford (eds) *Behaviour Modification for the Severely Retarded*. Amsterdam: Associated Scientific.

Hardy, L. (1999) 'Building blocks of reform', *The American School Board Journal*, February 1–11.

Miner, B. (1998) 'Reconstitution trend cools', *Rethinking Schools*, 13, 2, 118–35.

Orfield, G. (1996) 'Is reconstitution the answer for stuggling schools?', *The American School Board Journal*, February, 12–14.

Orfield, G. (2000) 'Wrong turn: the trouble with special measures', http://education.guardian.co.uk/print/0,3858,4039096,00.html

Rozmus, K. (1998) 'Education reform and education quality: is reconstitution the answer?', *BYU Education and Law Journal*, 4, 103–52.

8   Promoting High Expectations in Challenging Circumstances: Meanings, Evidence and Challenges for School Leaders

Louise Stoll and John MacBeath[1]

CHAPTER OVERVIEW

Louise Stoll and John MacBeath take the theme of school leadership as their contribution to this book. They suggest that it is convenient for governments to place responsibility for raising achievement on the school headteacher. In so doing, the locus of change is both personalized and locally defined. However, this also poses significant challenges to those individuals charged with such a task. In particular, it presents the leadership issue as a personalized one demanding heroic and sometimes superhuman skills. This may be of strategic value for governments, who have an easy means of locating blame if things go wrong, but it offers very little to the evolving community of the school where there is a demand perhaps for less razzmatazz and more concern for the careful weaving of the fabric of social, emotional and intellectual capital. The authors suggest that to do this demands a distribution of the question and process of leadership as a school wide, systemic challenge which draws upon individual strengths within a culture of high expectation. Their observation is particularly salient in the UK environment of recent times where 'superheads' have been placed into schools in difficulty (see also Chapter 2 by Terry Wrigley). The message here is subtle and different, drawing on Schein's work on leadership and culture where the leadership role is one of 'culture founding', Stoll and MacBeath remind us that there remains a significant need in challenging schools for the leadership to be distributed, both within school and then extending wider to the local support agencies, if there is to be a substantive longer-term effect which 'raises the game'.

When teacher expectations are discussed there is usually reference to Rosenthal and Jacobson's landmark 1968 study. While its findings are now attended with some reservation, the underlying premise is now beyond dispute: expectations matter. The evidence comes from psychology of perception – seeing what we expect to see (Asch, 1951), labelling theory – seeing where the label directs (Argyle, 1967), history and sociology of race and gender (Gillborn and Youdell, 2000; Weis and Fein, 2000), pupil voice research (Gow and Macpherson, 1970; Rudduck, 1996), neuropsychology (Kotulak, 1996; Greenfield, 2002), and two decades of school effectiveness research which has returned insistently to the theme of 'high expectations' as a critical variable in schools making more progress.

Indeed, school effectiveness research has had a major impact on government policy, internationally and nationally. In the UK, the Office for Standards in Education (Ofsted) commissioned a study to identify those features of schools that had proved to be most effective. Published in 1995, the report by Sammons and colleagues identified 11 key characteristics associated with greater effectiveness, including high expectations. Drawing on this review, schools in England are now inspected on a range of 'indicators', one of which is of high expectations. This encompasses judgements about whether targets are sufficiently challenging, the level of demands on pupils and the extent to which teachers: 'challenge pupils, expecting the most of them' (Ofsted, 2003: 30). This has been lent further impetus by a research carried out for the Department for Education and Employment by the consultants Hay McBer (DfEE, 2000), concluding that outstanding primary and secondary teachers have and communicate high expectations.

These studies, however, do not bring us much closer to how expectations are actually transmitted, operate and change. Nonetheless, governments around the world, spurred on by international league tables which point to wide disparities in attainment within and across nations, have exploited the growing evidence to urge schools and teachers to challenge their belief systems, to expect more from pupils and to set more ambitious targets. The impact on schools has been profound, in particular on schools in challenging circumstances for whom raising teacher and pupil expectations is often a critical variable but one that is embedded in a complex web of influences, historical, social and economic as well as educational.

It is in the context of these schools and these communities that we need to explore what 'expectations' means, what evidence we can adduce and what challenges there are for school leaders. The issues we raise in this chapter arise out of findings from a number of studies, in several of which one or both of us have been involved. These include: the Improving School Effectiveness Project in Scotland, commissioned by the then Scottish Office Education and Industry Department (SOEID) that took place from 1995 to 1998 (MacBeath and Mortimore, 2001); research from 2001 to 2002 evaluating the Implementation of the Key Stage 3 (11–14-year-olds) Strategy Pilot in England,[2] commissioned by the Department for Education and Skills (DfES); research currently underway on Schools in Exceptionally Challenging Circumstances, also commissioned by the Department for Education and Skills (DfES), from 2001 to 2004; and a four country study of effective leadership (MacBeath, 1998a).

What are 'expectations'?

A definition of expectations given by the New Shorter Oxford Dictionary is 'a preconceived idea of what will happen, what someone or something will turn out to be, etc.; the action of entertaining such an idea'. In relation to schools, Nash (1973) has suggested that 'somehow the teacher's mental attitudes to the child are ... being communicated'. This was the central thesis of the Rosenthal and Jacobson (1968) study which claimed that giving false information to teachers about a randomly selected group of 'intellectual bloomers' led to greater gains in IQ test scores for targeted children than for a group of control pupils because these teachers then 'expected' the 'bloomers' to do better and conveyed these expectations to all the pupils. Brophy and Good (1970) also documented the differential treatment of students in accordance with teachers' naturally occurring expectations.

As these and other studies have demonstrated, teachers' perceptions and actions are influenced by what they believe, as well as by their knowledge (Borko and Putnam, 1995). Reporting a study of four schools in low-income areas in New Zealand, Timperley and Robinson (2001: 282) describe how, despite data to the contrary, teachers explained pupils' poor academic achievement in terms of low-level entry skills, based on deeply embedded schema. These were articulated as sayings such as 'The children arrive at school with no skills', 'With their backgrounds, we cannot expect much progress in the first year'.

Teachers' understanding of expectations is not always clear. In a small study of one secondary school with a mixed catchment, encompassing an area of significant deprivation as well as pupils from more advantaged homes, questions to several staff members revealed a very narrow interpretation of the word 'expectations' (Fabara, 2001). These teachers discussed expectations in relation to pupil behaviour and were somewhat surprised when asked about academic expectations. This study took place prior to the Key Stage 3 Strategy (see below) and it is possible that understandings have changed.

So, through some kind of feedback loop, teachers' behaviours and attitudes communicate a message to their pupils about their ability, capability and behaviour. What, though, does this look like from the pupils' perspective?

Learning about expectations from pupils

Pupils know that success in school is important. For example, virtually all of the 2,164 Year 8 pupils surveyed as part of the Key Stage 3 Strategy Pilot evaluation felt that 'It is important for me to do well at school' (97 per cent) and that 'Getting good results is important to me' (96 per cent). Similarly, an overwhelming majority (97 per cent) believed that 'It is up to me to do the best I can', while almost as many (90 per cent) agreed that 'I think I could improve my school work'. These data suggest that pupils are well aware of what their schools expect of them but their assessment of their own competence in meeting those demands introduces a more complex chemistry. Their response to school, their engagement or disengagement, has to be understood in the light of their own perceptions of their ability, their expectations of success and fear of failure, and how these play out in school, classroom and community. Their motivation to learn is critical to achieving success (Weinstein, 1998) but largely dependent on what they expect of themselves, a self-identity shaped not only by teachers but even more powerfully by parents and peers (Harris, 1998).

The evidence suggests that a worrying number of pupils are 'disappointed', particularly in their adolescent years, expressing boredom when asked about their schooling (Rudduck *et al.*, 1996; Hargreaves *et al.*, 1996; McCall *et al.*, 2001). While boredom and disappointment may be explained in part by a failure of curriculum content and pedagogy, the ability to cope with boredom and to persist in the face of failure and setback appears to be related to expectations to how pupils see themselves as learners. These researchers identified two kinds of responses to a difficult task. One was to meet the challenge and to rise above the occasion. The other was to turn inwards to blame themselves, a 'helpless response' measuring their own personal worth and intelligence against the task, willing to settle for the explanation that they just weren't clever enough. The task itself was then blamed for being 'stupid', or 'boring'.

There is confirmation for these findings in Bandura's (1986) work on self-efficacy. He found that individuals with high self-efficacy beliefs exerted greater effort during difficult tasks, suffered less stress in taxing situations and chose more challenging goals to sustain their interest and involvement. In contrast, those with low self-efficacy beliefs reduced their effort, tended to give up when faced with difficult tasks, emphasized their own personal deficiencies, developed avoidance behaviour, experienced increased anxiety and stress and were more likely to lower their aspirations. As Crooks (1988: 462) explains:

> The main mechanism for building self-efficacy in a particular domain appears to be experiencing repeated success on tasks in that domain. Success at tasks perceived to be difficult or challenging is more influential than success on easier tasks. On the other hand, of course, repeated failure leads to lowered self-efficacy.

An appropriate level of challenge is important to pupils. Most (71 per cent) of the Year 8 pupils surveyed as part of the KS3 Pilot evaluation reported that 'I like work that challenges me'. In contrast small, but not insignificant, percentages of pupils thought that either 'My work is too easy for me' (18 per cent) or 'My work is too hard for me' (14 per cent). Furthermore, a higher percentage of pupils in lower achieving schools (23 per cent) – classified by school achievement at KS3 and related to indicators of deprivation – than higher achieving schools (13 per cent) reported that 'My work is too easy for me'. When asked to describe what helps them to learn at school, answers provide elaboration:

> When my teachers sets work that I may not find easy but I understand clearly and that I can work out.
> Being pushed and maybe even doing harder/easier things than my classmates which doesn't happen.
> I like work that challenges me, but when teachers help me understand it before hand, and can help if I get stuck on anything.
> Teachers that encourage me and tell me that I can do better.

How pupils cope with challenge has also been explored by Csikszentmihalyi (1997), confirming that achieving the right level of challenge is critical to success. As this varies considerably from one individual to the next, it presents the class teacher with a delicate balance to achieve. Based on a study of thousands of children, young people and adults Csikszentmihalyi (1977: 29) concluded:

> If challenges are too high one gets frustrated, then worried, and eventually anxious. If challenges are too low relative to one's skills one gets relaxed, then bored. If both challenges and skills are perceived to be low, one gets to feel apathetic.

Further evidence for this is provided by an English study of young people who achieved grades D–G in a system where A–C are seen as the pass grades. Students entered for this tier had a lowered sense of self-efficacy (Gillborn and Youdell, 2000). We are left to puzzle over issues of cause and effect, but in the process we are learning more and more from research studies about how pupils respond to feedback whether to their contribution in class, the evaluation of their work by the teacher, or the impact of testing on their self-belief and ability. What pupils are told about themselves and their work, and the way in which teachers give feedback has been shown to be a significant determinant of whether they progress, stall or regress in their effort and achievement (Kluger and DeNisi, 1996; Black and Wiliam, 1998). What Black and Wiliam's research shows, confirmed by a recent study by Gipps and colleagues (2000), is that feedback when positive, specific and formative, raises expectations and achievement.

The message from these studies is that teachers can be surprised into higher expectations given evidence of what their pupils can achieve when provided with appropriate stimulus or 'scaffolding' (Vygotsky, 1978). However, a deeper shift in belief systems about 'ability' and 'potential' is likely to take longer.

Changing teachers' expectations

The self-efficacy of teachers and their own confidence to feel they can make a difference and achieve the results they desire appears as critical as that of pupils, and is a central influence on their orientation to learning (Stoll, 1999) as well as their willingness and ability to change. Confident teachers seem to believe that what they do can, and does, make a significant difference to their pupils' progress and development. They have a sense of pride in, and certainty about, their work. In Rosenholtz's (1989: 318) words, this helps them learn and grow, making them 'more likely to persevere, to define problem students as a challenge, to seek outside resources to conquer that challenge, and, in this way, to actually foster students' academic gains'.

A large body of work exists to indicate that belief change during adulthood occurs relatively rarely (see review in Pajares, 1992). But, as Fullan (2001) contends, changes in teachers' behaviour and practices can change what they believe, this occurs once teachers are convinced that their actions have made a positive difference. This is the message of studies on assessment for learning (Gipps *et al.*, 2000; Wiliam and Lee, 2001; Swaffield and Dudley, 2002) and has clearly been an intent of the Key Stage 3 Strategy. One of its four principles is: 'establishing high expectations for all pupils and setting challenging targets for them to achieve'.

Schools in the Strategy Pilot were provided with draft curriculum frameworks for mathematics, English and science and teachers given training in the setting of achievement targets. A clearer focus on objectives, it was hoped, would support teachers in raising expectations, a strategy that seems, for the most part, to have had a positive impact. Visits to pilot schools suggested that objectives were helping to focus teachers' work more clearly. As one head of English explained:

> The sharing of objectives has helped particularly boys and staff to think about why they are doing what they are doing.

Sometimes this appeared to be because objectives had made them realize that expectations were previously too low. For example, a head of science noted:

> We've pretty much accepted that we underestimated what kids could do at KS2.

At other times, departments and schools were clearly responding to external pressures:

> The English department now feels under more pressure to deliver results. (headteacher)
>   We have had the pressures of a dip in results and competition from other schools so I am target setting very closely. (headteacher)

A key finding of the Key Stage 3 Strategy Pilot research was a pattern of increased expectations in lower-achieving schools. When teachers responding to the teacher survey were classified in relation to the percentage of their schools' pupils on free school meals (FSM), differences emerged between schools in teachers' responses to the item 'The KS3 Pilot has led me to set more challenging targets for my pupils'. While average agreement was 59 per cent, substantially more teachers from high free school meals (FSM) schools (79 per cent in schools with 35 per cent and more FSM) agreed than those in low FSM schools (35 per cent in schools with 0–5 per cent FSM). It is, of course, possible that the pronounced differences may stem from teachers in high-achieving schools, with low FSM percentages, being more likely to claim that they already set demanding targets.

Some of the schools and LEAs appeared to be struggling with target setting, a process that pre-dated the Pilot (DfEE, 1998). They either set targets that were too high or low, or found the data they had was inadequate. Some schools with greater prior experience of target setting, however, appeared to use the Pilot to move towards more individualized pupil targets, involving the pupils more in the process and attempting to raise their aspirations. Overall 61 per cent of the Year 8 pupils surveyed thought 'Having targets helps me improve my work'. This was more characteristic of pupils in lower-achieving schools (66 per cent) than higher-achieving schools (56 per cent). In lower-achieving schools targets were also set more frequently. Pupils in one school in a disadvantaged area commented:

> They set targets in tests: it gives you something to work at. (Year 8)
>> Targets help evaluate how you can improve (Year 9)
>> They're helpful because they are guides, and you can follow and see how well you are doing. (Year 9)

Pupils, however, differed in their understanding of, and liking for, targets. Those who reported receiving extra help were more likely to express a preference for targets than pupils not receiving help (79 per cent as compared to 59 per cent). This preference for targets may be linked to views expressed by the Year 8 pupils that what helped their learning most was clarity about what they are learning and what they needed to do. Lower-attaining pupils may well have less understanding of the purposes of their learning and what is required of them in lessons (Rudduck, 1996).

Raising of teacher expectations in the Key Stage 3 Strategy Pilot may be reflected in a relatively high level of agreement (74 per cent) with the survey statement: 'Teachers in this school believe all pupils can be successful'. Over the last decade, this item has been included in a number of other surveys of teachers of pupils in the middle years (for example, Muschamp *et al.*, 2001) and secondary pupils (for example, McCall *et al.*, 2001), with significantly fewer teachers agreeing with the statement. It appears, therefore, that this Pilot, in combination with other initiatives, for example target setting, may have had an impact on raising expectations, particularly in relation to lower-attaining pupils. This is supported by a significant difference between pupils in a matched sample of pilot and non-pilot schools when responding to the survey item 'My work is too hard for me'. While 12 per cent of those in non-pilot schools felt their work was too hard for them, 20 per cent of pupils in pilot schools believed this to be true.

In general, these results seem to suggest that it is possible for an external reform effort to have an impact on teacher expectations in areas of deprivation. Questions, however, remain. To what extent have expectations really be raised? Is this adequate to help schools in challenging circumstances move forwards on an upward improvement trajectory? To what extent is this sustainable in areas of serious deprivation? This brings us to the issue of context and what 'high expectations' means in different contexts.

A matter of context

One of the most important lessons we have learned is that expectations do not operate in some kind of social or cultural vacuum but are heavily dependent on context and history. Results from comparative studies, most recently the OECD PISA report (2001), are often treated unproblematically, policy-makers in many countries either claiming evidence of successful policy implementation or blaming schools for low standards. Yet we know enough about expectations, in the culture, in families, in schools and in young people themselves to be wary of attributing success simply to structural factors, classroom methodology or the aspirations of classroom teachers and school headteachers.

When thinking about expectations, it is vital to consider the socio-economic context of the school, not simply in terms of proxy indicators such as free meal entitlement, but also in terms of the peculiar character of disadvantaged communities. Disadvantage may express itself quite differently in rural and urban areas but these are not homogeneous categories. Urban disadvantage takes significantly different forms in multi-ethnic communities and predominantly white working-class communities. Within London, for example, different boroughs present different kinds of social compositions and educational challenges. The more we research, the more we find that there is no simple causal relationship between social disadvantage and school achievement. There is growing evidence of what schools in challenging circumstances can do to significantly raise attainment, but we are still some way from producing robust evidence on the sustainability of such gains and how expectations are raised in the short and longer term. Are strategies context specific or are there more general principles that can be adduced? Are there forces at work in the most turbulent of communities that require very specific kinds of intervention and even radically different forms of educational provision?

A current research study involving schools in 'extremely challenging circumstances' (Cullen, 2003) describes aspects of their communities which seriously constrain what they are able to achieve. An overriding theme is poverty and what is contained, and what is not contained, within that descriptive envelope. Poverty is associated with ill health and chronic illness stemming from psychological, social and dietary factors, sub-standard housing and maintenance, compounded by unemployment, transient relationships and domestic turbulence. These factors lay vulnerable families open to exploitation, drug abuse and the twilight economy, what Manuel Castells (1997) describes as 'perverse integration'; that is, routes back into the economy through illegal trading and theft.

Violence, extortion and territorial warfare follow in the wake of illegal traffic causing flight of the most advantaged and resilient of families into other neighbourhoods. As vacant housing is occupied by immigrants and refugees, violence assumes a racist dimension.

These conditions have a far-reaching impact on the life of the school, the classroom and the motivation and engagement of individual pupils. The social mix within their peer group does not offer models to emulate or obvious incentives to work hard. Homework and learning out of school are equally compromised without parental support and encouragement, counterposed with more attractive distractions, including part-time work (legal and illegal). It is difficult for learning to be sustained out of school without adequate space – physical, social or intellectual. It is also often difficult for the kind of experiential learning that takes place in community and peer group to be acknowledged or celebrated in school. Furthermore, some young people live in homes where parents have low aspirations for their children, as described by staff in several of our projects, including those who do not see any benefits for the future of their children taking school leaving examinations.

The influence of peers

The peer group, as every teacher knows, exerts a profound influence on attitudes to school, to classroom learning and to expectations of success. Teachers are the first to recognize that learning is not simply a product of what takes place between two individuals, teacher and pupil, but is mediated by the social context in which different sets of expectations are at work. They understand at first hand what effectiveness studies have come to call the 'contextual' or 'compositional' effect (Willms, 1985; Croxford and Cowie, 1996; MacBeath and Mortimore, 2001). This is the effect that the expectations of the peer group exercises on the individual pupils, often a powerful counter force to that of the teacher. It is what Thrupp (1999) describes in his study of social mix, illustrating how difficult this is to disentangle from other school effects. It is 'compositional' because it may assume a critical mass, a component of classroom or school so dynamic that it drags down achievement across the school. Judith Harris (1998), writing in the United States context, makes a powerful case for the importance of peer group expectations. She sees these operating more powerfully than those of family and teachers. She argues, with reference to a substantial body of research, that a child's identity as a person, her capacity as a learner and expectation as a pupil, come from the way in which she defines herself within the immediate peer reference group. The categories we use in our analysis – sex, race, ability, class – may or may not be salient characteristics of children's identity, she argues, but only assume significance when school structures and the nature of the school social mix push these features into social prominence.

It is in challenging social and economic circumstances that the peer effect is most likely to work at cross grain to the values and expectations of the school. Since the classic studies of anti-learning cultures identified by Hargreaves (1967) and Willis (1977), studies in Britain (Riley and Rustique-Forrester, 2002) and in the USA (Weis and Fine, 2000) have continued to document the uphill struggle for schools and teachers.

Schools can have different expectations

Despite the contextual challenges we have identified, those working in schools with ostensibly similar catchments often have very different expectations of pupils. The operation of expectations at whole-school level is taken as axiomatic by governments' charge against failing schools and, in England, Ofsted's categorization of high expectations, as well by researchers exploring school ethos and culture. As we know from our Scottish study, the Improving School Effectiveness Project (ISEP) (MacBeath and Mortimore, 2001), two schools with very similar intakes can have completely different collective beliefs about their pupils. Compare, for example, these comments from teachers in two of the participating primary schools. Both serve areas of serious deprivation. Teachers were asked 'What are the most significant factors affecting children's ability to learn?' The response in one school was:

> Home background, deprivation, parental views on education. Often survival is more important than taking on board educational opportunities.
> Some children are never going to achieve very much.

In contrast, in the other school, the response was:

> there are no limitations. You can come in this door and the world is your oyster ... the children will be encouraged. Nothing is holding them back.

These comments were not individually held but appeared to characterize a shared value system. One teacher who described the pupils as 'vulnerable and they have to be able to cope with what they are doing', was also very clear that 'it doesn't mean that you don't push them further the next time', adding emphatically: 'If they are going to learn ... they will learn here.' A colleague echoed these same firm beliefs: 'Everyone wants the children to achieve great things.'

Eighty-eight per cent of teachers at this school agreed with a survey statement that teachers in this school believe all pupils can be successful, compared with 50 per cent in the other school and 73 per cent for the whole primary teacher sample (Stoll *et al.*, 2001). In one secondary school involved in the same project hardly any teachers agreed with the same statement (MacBeath, 1998b).

This evidence suggests that, even in extremely challenging areas, there are differences at a whole-school level in the culture of expectations. How these aspects of whole-school culture play out at classroom level has been largely neglected in research. However, we hope to learn more from a collaborative project among four universities (Cambridge, King's College (London), Reading and the Open University) currently studying those connections. Its focus, Learning How to Learn, is exploring that concept at pupil, teacher and school level, building on the ISEP survey described above, but probing further the inter-relationship of school and classroom dynamic (www.learntolearn.ac.uk). What evidence there is, suggests Weinstein (1998: 104–5):

> highlights the reciprocal relationship between the working and learning
> conditions for teachers and the learning context for students in classrooms.
> Consistent, stimulating, and supportive conditions for school staff to
> question their expectations for students – not only in addressing beliefs
> about ability but also in examining teaching practices and policies – were
> critical in promoting a positive expectancy climate.

Sarason (1990), in similar vein, concluded that: 'it is virtually impossible to create and sustain over time conditions for productive learning for students when they do not exist for teachers'. While we believe the links between organizational learning and pupil learning to be self-evident, there is little evidence so far to demonstrate that inherent expectations – 'how organisations work when no one is looking' (Morgan, 1997) – have a direct impact on achievement. Margaret Thatcher once famously declared that there was an inverse correlation between a school's emphasis on caring and its levels of achievement. Throughout her period of office, and carried through by successive governments, the criticism of softness has been levelled, in particular, at schools in areas of deprivation. Caring may be patronizing, and a 'welfarist' culture (Hargreaves, 1995) a weak substitute for an achievement culture, but it is a needlessly false dichotomy. A contrasting view of caring:

> requires expectations of quality work from all children. To do less is
> uncaring. To decide that pupils cannot learn important things, like reading,
> because they are deprived, handicapped in some way or not academically

bright, is to be uncaring and inhumane. Caring teachers expect all pupils to do well; they do what it takes to the best of their abilities to help each pupil achieve. The same principles of caring that engage pupils in their learning apply equally to caring for teachers, for parents, for important ideas, or for organizations like schools. (Stoll and Fink, 1996: 192)

Caring by this definition is neither self-indulgent nor permissive but made of sterner stuff. When asked about the qualities of good teachers, a group of secondary students made a distinction between 'teachers who were strict for themselves as against "strict for you", those "who make you do it" and "those you do it for because you know they care for you"' (MacBeath, 1998a: 61). When they spoke about teachers 'who make you feel clever' (p. 60) they were implicitly recognizing a process in brain chemistry that comes into play when there is a supportive but challenging relationship.

Pulling it all together: the challenge for school leaders

Responsibility for raising expectations is increasingly seen by governments as lying at the door of the school's headteacher. Headteachers, it is believed, can instill an ethic of achievement, drawing on their own inspirational and heroic qualities. It is a belief that has appealed to governments, drawing for evidence on countless studies which have found positive leadership to be a powerful force for school improvement and school effectiveness (see Mortimore, 1998; Teddlie and Reynolds, 2000). What this means in different countries has been less researched.

A recent four-country study (Denmark, Australia, England and Scotland) illustrated the extent to which different leadership strategies may be required not only in different national cultures but also in schools within countries (MacBeath, 1998a). Headteachers who moved from one school to another also found that they had to develop different ways of being. Similar findings come from the United States in different socio-economic contexts (Hallinger and Murphy, 1986; Teddlie and Stringfield, 1993). However, research has left many questions unanswered as to the inter-relationship of expectations between the school and the community.

While in many different cultural contexts research tends to find a correlation between attainment levels and qualities of leadership, there is a question about direct effects, as opposed to indirect, or mediated, effects. In the Tasmanian context, for example, Silins and Mulford (2002) conclude that leadership cannot be shown directly to effect student outcomes but that achievement levels improve when leadership sources are distributed throughout the school community and where teachers are empowered in areas of importance to them. Leaders have been described as the 'culture founders' (Schein, 1985; Nias *et al.*, 1989), and that the 'only thing of real importance that leaders do is to create and manage culture' (Schein, 1985: 2).

Creating and managing a culture of achievement for all pupils' progress is likely to include the following:

- the ways leaders model their own expectations and challenge low expectations of others (Mortimore *et al.*, 2000);
- how leaders use data to challenge low expectations where they occur, including differential expectations of certain groups of pupils (Earl and Lee, 1998; Southworth and Conner, 1999).
- how school leaders' feedback to teachers influences expectations;
- how school leaders deal with low aspirations on the part of pupils and their parents, where these occur.

Evans' (1999) research in primary schools, although not specifically schools in challenging circumstances, highlights how some school leaders motivate teachers in their schools to excel. As one teacher said of her head: 'I don't know what it is about her, but she made you want to do your best ... she suddenly made you realize what was possible, and you, kind of, raised your game all the time' (p. 18).

'Raising your game' is likely to be at its most critical in schools in circumstances where there are extra layers of challenge, not only from embattled communities but also relentless pressure from government to raise standards year on year. In these schools it is not only unreasonable but also disempowering to expect teachers individually and autonomously to raise their own game. The game, in these circumstances, has to be a team effort. It has to be one in which teachers have a tangible sense of support from their leaders and their colleagues. It is about capacity building so that schools as communities share optimism and resilience in the face of setbacks. There is no evidence to suggest, however, that disadvantaged schools can go it alone. Indeed there is much evidence to the contrary. As we have found in our research (Stoll *et al.*, 2001) schools need friends. They need friends on the ground who both support and challenge. They need friends in their communities – social and community agencies, voluntary agencies, parent coalitions and local media. They also need friends in high places – local authorities, government and universities, who not only understand but invest in partnerships.

Expectations matter. There are few who would dispute that simple aphorism. We do need, however, to be careful neither to over simplify nor over mystify its impact and effects. We have learned much but there remains a lot still to learn.

Notes

1 With thanks to members of the research teams of the projects discussed in this chapter.
2 The Key Stage 3 Strategy is a major government initiative to raise standards for 11 to 14-year-olds, in the light of considerable evidence that many pupils in this age group do not make sufficient progress. The Strategy has been designed to raise standards by enhancing teaching and learning practices, based on good practice, supported by materials, training and other resources. The evaluation looked at the Pilot of the Strategy, which has been rolled out on a national basis.

References

Argyle, M. (1967) *The Psychology of Interpersonal Behaviour*: Harmondsworth: Penguin.

Asch, S.E. (1951) 'Effects of group pressure on the distortion and modification of judgements', in J. Guetzkow (ed.) *Groups, Leadership and Men*. Pittsburgh, PA: Rutgers University Press.

Bandura, A. (1986) *Social Foundations of Thought and Action: A Social Cognitive Theory*. Englewood Cliffs, NJ: Prentice Hall.

Black, P. and Wiliam, D. (1998) *Beyond the Black Box*. London: Kings College.

Borko, H. and Putnam, R. T. (1995) 'Expanding a teacher's knowledge base: a cognitive psychological perspective on professional development', in T. R. Guskey and M. Huberman (eds) *Professional Development in Education: New Paradigms & Practices*. New York: Teachers College Press.

Brophy, J. E. and Good, T. L. (1970) 'Teachers' communication of differential expectations for children's classroom performance: some behavioral data', *Journal of Educational Psychology*, 61, 365–74.

Castells, M. (1997) *End of Millennium*. Oxford: Blackwell.

Crooks, T. J. (1988) 'The impact of classroom evaluation practices on students', *Review of Educational Research*, 58, 438–81.

Croxford L. and Cowie, L. (1996) *The Effectiveness of Grampian Secondary Schools*. Grampian Regional Council, Edinburgh: Centre for Educational Sociology.

Cullen, J. (2003) 'Building capacity in "struggling" schools'. Paper presented at the Sixteenth International Congress for School Effectiveness and Improvement, Sydney, January 5–8.

Csikszentmihalyi, M. (1997) *Living Well: The Psychology of Everyday Life*. London: Weidenfeld & Nicholson.

DfEE (1998) *Target-setting in Schools: Guidance for Headteachers and Governing Bodies*. Suffolk: DfEE Publications.

DfEE (2000) *A Model of Teacher Effectiveness: Report by Hay McBer to the Department for Education and Employment – June 2000*. London: DfEE.

Earl, L. and Lee, L. (1998) *Evaluation of the Manitoba School Improvement Program*. Toronto: Walter and Duncan Gordon Foundation.

Evans, L. (1999) *Managing to Motivate: A Guide for School Leaders*. London: Cassell.

Fabara, P. (2001) 'A case study of the role of the headteacher in raising teachers' expectations'. University of Bath: unpublished Masters Dissertation.

Fullan, M. (2001) *The New Meaning of Educational Change*. London: RoutledgeFalmer.

Gillborn, D. and Youdell, D. (2000) *Rationing Education: Policy, Practice Reform and Equity*, Buckingham: Open University Press.

Gipps, C., McCallum, B. and Hargreaves, E. (2000) *What Makes a Good Primary School Teacher? Expert Classroom Strategies*. London: RoutledgeFalmer.

Hallinger, P. and Murphy, J. (1986) 'The social context of effective schools', *American Journal of Education*, 94, 3, 328–55.

Hargreaves, A., Earl, L. and Ryan, J. (1996) *Schooling for Change: Reinventing Education for Early Adolescents*. London: Falmer Press.

Hargreaves D. H. (1967) *Social Relations in a Secondary School*, London: Routledge and Kegan Paul.

Hargreaves, D. (1995) 'School culture, school effectiveness and school improvement', *School Effectiveness and School Improvement*, 6, 1, 23–46.

Harris, J. R. (1998) *The Nurture Assumption*. London: Bloomsbury.

Kluger, A.V. and Denisi, A. (1996) 'The effects of feedback interventions on performance: a historical review, a meta-analysis, and a preliminary feedback intervention theory', *Psychological Bulletin*, 119, 2, 252–84.

Kotulak, R. (1996) *Inside the Brain: Revolutionary Discoveries of How the Mind Works*. Kansas City: Andrews McMeel.

MacBeath, J. (ed.) (1998a) *Effective School Leadership: Responding to Change*. London: Paul Chapman.

MacBeath, J. (1998b) ' "I didn't know he was ill": the role and value of the critical friend', in L. Stoll and K. Myers (eds) *No Quick Fixes: Perspectives on Schools in Difficulty*. London: Falmer Press.

MacBeath, J. and Mortimore, P. (2001) *Improving School Effectiveness*. Buckingham: Open University Press.

McCall, J., Smith, I., Stoll, L., Thomas, S., Sammons, P., Smees, R., MacBeath, J., Boyd, B. and McGilchrist, B. (2001) 'Views of pupils, parents and teachers: vital indicators of effectiveness and for improvement', in J. MacBeath and P. Mortimore (eds) *Improving School Effectiveness*. Buckingham: Open University Press.

Mortimore, P. (1998) *The Road to Improvement: Reflections on School Effectiveness*. Lisse, the Netherlands: Swets & Zeitlinger.

Mortimore, P., Gopinathan, S., Leo, E., Myers, K., Sharpe, L., Stoll, L. and Mortimore, J. (2000) *The Culture of Change: Case Studies of Improving Schools in Singapore and London*. London: Bedford Way Papers.

Muschamp, Y., Stoll, L. and Nausheen, M. (2001) 'Learning in the middle years', in C. W. Day and D. Van Veen (eds) *Educational Research in Europe Yearbook 2001*. Leuven, Belgium: Garant.

Morgan, G. (1997) *Images of Organization*. Thousand Oaks, CA and London: Sage.

Nash, R. (1973) *Classrooms Observed: The Teacher's Perception and Pupil's Performance*. London: Routledge and Kegan Paul.

Nias, J., Southworth, G. and Yeomans, R. (1989) *Staff Relationships in the Primary School: A Study of Organizational Cultures*. London: Cassell.

OECD (2001) *Knowledge and Skills for Life: First Results From PISA 2000*. Paris: OECD.

Ofsted (2003) *Inspecting Schools: The Framework for Inspecting Schools in England from September 2003*. London: Office for Standards in Education.

Pajares, M. F. (1992) 'Teachers' beliefs and educational research: cleaning up a messy construct', *Review of Educational Research*, 62, 3, 307–32.

Riley, K. and Rustique-Forrester, E. (2002) *Working with Disaffected Students*. London: Paul Chapman.

Rosenholtz, S. J. (1989) *Teachers' Workplace: The Social Organization of Schools*. New York: Longman.

Rosenthal, R. and Jacobson, L. (1968) *Pygmalion in the Classroom*. New York: Holt, Rinehart and Winston.

Ruddock, J. (1996) 'Lessons, subjects and the curriculum issues of "understanding" and "coherence" ', in J. Ruddock, R. Chaplain and

G. Wallace (eds) *School Improvement: What Can Pupils Tell Us?* London: David Fulton.

Rudduck, J., Chaplain, R. and Wallace, G. (1996) *School Improvement: What Can Pupils Tell Us?* London: David Fulton.

Sammons, P., Hillman, J. and Mortimore, P. (1995) *Key Characteristics of Effective Schools: a Review of School Effectiveness Research.* London: Office for Standards in Education.

Sarason, S. B. (1990) *The Predictable Failure of Educational Reform.* San Francisco: Jossey-Bass.

Schein, E. H. (1985) *Organizational Culture and Leadership.* San Francisco: Jossey-Bass.

Silins, H. and Mulford, B. (2002) 'Leadership and organisational outcomes', in K. Liethwood and P. Hallinger (eds) *Second International Handbook of Educational Leadership and Administration.* Amsterdam: Kluwer.

Southworth, G. and Conner, C. (1999) *Managing Improving Primary Schools: Using Evidence-based Management and Leadership.* London: Falmer.

Stoll, L. (1999) 'Realising our potential: understanding and developing capacity for lasting improvement', *School Effectiveness and School Improvement,* 10, 4, 503–35.

Stoll, L. and Fink, D. (1996) *Changing Our Schools: Linking School Effectiveness and School Improvement.* Buckingham: Open University Press.

Stoll, L., MacBeath, J. and Mortimore, B. (2001) 'Beyond 2000: where next for effectiveness and improvement?' in J. MacBeath and P. Mortimore (eds) *Improving School Effectiveness.* Buckingham: Open University Press.

Swaffield, S. and Dudley, P. (2002) *Assessment Literacy for Wise Decisions.* London: Association of Teachers and Lecturers.

Teddlie, C. and Reynolds, D. (2000) *International Handbook of School Effectiveness Research.* London: Falmer Press.

Teddlie, C. and Stringfield, S. (1993) *Schools Make a Difference: Lessons Learned from a 10 Year Study of School Effects.* New York: Teachers College Press.

Thomas, S., Smees, R. and Boyd, B. (1998) *Valuing Pupils' Views in Scottish Schools: Policy Paper No. 3.* London University: Institute of Education.

Thrupp, M. (1999) *Schools Making a Difference: Let's Be Realistic.* Buckingham: Open University Press.

Timperley, H. S. and Robinson, V. M. J. (2001) 'Achieving school improvement through challenging and changing teachers' schema', *Journal of Educational Change,* 2, 281–300.

Vygotsky, L. S. (1978) *Mind in Society: The Development of the Higher Psychological Processes.* Cambridge, MA: Harvard University Press. (Originally published in 1930, New York: Oxford University Press.)

Weinstein, R. S. (1998) 'Promoting positive expectations in schooling', in N. M. Lambert and B. L. McCombs (eds) *How Students Learn: Reforming Schools Through Learner-Centered Education.* Washington, DC: American Psychological Association.

Weis, L. and Fine, M. (2000) *Construction Sites: Excavating Race, Class and Gender among Urban Youth.* New York: Teachers College Press.

Willis, P. (1977) *Learning to Labour: How Working-Class Kids get Working-Class Jobs.* London: Gower.

Wiliam, D. and Lee, C. (2001) 'Teachers developing assessment for learning: impact on student achievement'. Paper presented at British Educational Research Association 27th Annual Conference held at University of Leeds. September. London, UK: King's College London School of Education.

Willms, J. D. (1985) 'The balance thesis – contextual effects of ability on pupils "O" grade examination results', *Oxford Review of Education,* 11, 1, 33–41.

9 Raising Attainment in Schools Serving Communities with High Levels of Socio-Economic Disadvantage: The Experience of a School in a Former Coalfield Area

Christopher Chapman and Jen Russ

CHAPTER OVERVIEW

An observation from many of the authors in this book is that schools in difficulty often reside in places of considerable urban deprivation and poverty.
This chapter from Chris Chapman and Jen Russ report a programme of
intervention and support in a former coalfield area. The authors describe
the presenting issues arising from a series of interviews with teaching staff
working in schools from which they then describe interventions designed to
have a positive effect. Whilst there were clearly resource-rich related interventions taking place, what is perhaps most noticeable is the discussion
of the sustainability of the programmes and the significance of emotional
support as a basis for programme sustainability. The authors report that
adherence to simplistic technical and often policy-led approaches on their
own are likely to fail to engage participants.

Introduction

Recently, low-attaining schools and schools serving communities with
high levels of socio-economic deprivation have been given much attention
on the national and international stage by both policy-makers and
researchers alike. While schools in the Department for Education and
Skills (DfES) 'challenging circumstances' category[1] vary considerably,
schools in low socio-economic status (SES) areas, schools in urban
contexts, schools with falling roles and schools serving inner-city populations are over-represented in this group (Gray, 2000). Evidence indicates
that schools that are facing challenging circumstances tend to perform
at educational levels that are at or below the national average. This is
a trend reflected in schools in the former coalfield areas where many of
the characteristics of social and economic deprivation are in evidence

and where educational attainment consistently lags behind national standards.

Since the early 1980s, the former coalfield regions have experienced a range of changes that have culminated in declining standards of living and in reduced levels of pupil performance and attainment. The research study commissioned by the DfES, 'Patterns of Educational Attainment in the British Coalfields' (Gore and Smith, 2001), demonstrated the extent of this problem by highlighting the disparity in pupil attainment in schools in this particular context. However, this research also highlighted that pupil under-achievement was not the result of a particular 'coalfield effect' but that the prevailing set of socio-economic factors were directly linked to low levels of academic performance.

The school effectiveness and school improvement literatures both reiterate the importance of social disadvantage upon levels of pupil performance and achievement (Sammons *et al.*, 1997; Sammons, 1999; Teddlie and Reynolds, 2000; Stoll and Fink, 1996; Hopkins, 2001a; Harris *et al.*, 2003). This research evidence shows that the most important factor influencing educational outcomes is pupil prior attainment and that socio-economic status and occupation directly influences levels of prior attainment (Gray, 2000). The home background, therefore, has a significant effect upon the subsequent educational achievement of young people. However, while it is an important variable, it is not the only factor that affects levels of performance and achievement.

The school effectiveness research identifies a range of school-related factors that influence school performance and demonstrates that 'these are open to modification by staff rather than fixed by external constraints' (Rutter, 1979: 273). This research tradition suggests that even schools in the most difficult circumstances can reach acceptable levels of academic achievement and performance (see, for example Teddlie and Stringfield, 1993; Hallinger and Murphy, 1986; Evans and Teddlie, 1995; Maden, 2001). The school effectiveness and school improvement research base also demonstrates that pupil and school performance can be enhanced irrespective of school context or socio-economic factors. Recent research focused upon schools that are improving in difficult circumstances has explored how schools in difficult contexts can improve and how pupils in these schools attain acceptable levels of academic achievement (Harris *et al.*, 2003).

Therefore, evidence suggests that schools in difficult socio-economic circumstances can improve and can sustain that improvement over time (e.g., Elmore, 2000; Louis and Marks, 1996; Louis and Miles, 1990). Researchers in England have recently focused their attention upon improving schools in difficulty or challenging contexts and illustrated how improvement occurs over time (e.g. Stoll and Myers, 1998; Hopkins *et al.*, 1997; Barber and Dann, 1996; Gray, 2000; National Commission on Education, 1996). Recent work in this area has highlighted the possibility of improving attainment in schools in low socio-economic contexts and provided insights into the processes that can lead to school-level development and improved pupil performance (e.g., Reynolds *et al.*, 2001; Hopkins, 2001b).

This chapter is a response to the call for further case studies that investigate the processes that lead to improvement in the most difficult of contexts (Maden, 2001). It draws on research findings commissioned by the DfES into schools that have successfully raised attainment in former coalfield areas (Harris *et al.*, 2003). First, the context and presenting issues are explored. Second, the school's overarching framework for improvement presented. Third, examples of core strategies for improvement that have been employed to deliver year-on-year improvement over a five-year period are discussed. In conclusion, speculations are made regarding the key elements for improving such schools and the extent to which improvement strategies are transferable between individual schools and different contexts are made.

A brief note on method

The case described in this chapter is drawn from research into eight schools in the Department for Education and Skills (DfES) 'Raising Attainment in Former Coalfield Areas' project. All quotations in this chapter illustrate important themes, findings and conclusions drawn from the wider group of eight schools. Criteria for selection of schools for this project included year-on-year improvement over a five-year period in GCSE examination performance and scrutiny of documentary evidence that suggested that improvement had been made in a range of areas. Semi-structured interviews were conducted with teaching staff at all levels. In addition, focus groups of Year 9 students were interviewed and asked to complete questionnaires. Interviews were recorded with a digital recorder and data were coded using anotape software. Emerging themes and trends were identified in two-dimensional matrices and selective transcriptions used as a basis for direct quotations. Inevitably, as with any small-scale project the scope for widespread generalization is limited. However, careful attention to internal validity of the process and the nature of the findings provide helpful insights into the improvement of a group of schools that, to date, have been paid little attention by researchers or policy-makers.

School X: a pathway to sustainable improvement?

Context

School X is situated in a former colliery village in the centre of the former Yorkshire coalfield. Since the colliery closure programme and the demise of associated support industries the area has suffered from increased levels of socio-economic deprivation and a declining population. However, more recently attempts have been made to reverse this trend with the introduction of a ten-year regeneration programme. This has included the opening of a business and support centre and the development of an ongoing commitment to the concept of life-long learning. Unfortunately attempts at regeneration remain limited and successes appear to be challenging to deliver.

Within this dynamic and challenging context School X has embarked on a passage of significant change during the last ten years. It is a school that has risen to the initial challenges presented by Ofsted during the first round of inspections. It is an improving school, experiencing year-on-year increases in pupil performance at GCSE at a rate better than national or LEA averages (see Figure 9.1). Progress has also been made in other areas including the reduction in absence rates (see Figure 9.2) and improved student behaviour. It is a school that serves a predominantly European Caucasian community with pockets of extreme levels of socio-economic deprivation. However, the intake is comprehensive but significantly skewed towards students from low socio-economic backgrounds with, as one would expect, low levels of prior attainment; a situation that has not dramatically changed in recent years (Ofsted, 2003).

Culturally, School X could be described as a moving school (Rozenholtz, 1989) with an upward trajectory. It is a hothouse of activity within a fluid, rapidly changing environment and consequently, all individuals must be flexible in approach and willing to participate. Teachers in this school possess extremely high levels of energy and an uncompromising approach to improving student's life chances. Formal (Hargreaves, 1997) tendencies can be identified within this hothouse environment. Competitive sports are encouraged, there are trophy cabinets displaying intra-school cups and prizes. The underpinning values of adults within the school could be described as 'traditional' where the expectation is that all individuals will give their all. This goes beyond the school into the community and perhaps, ironically in a climate of high unemployment, is exemplified by the work ethic of 'work hard and play hard' in a traditional sense. Traditional boundaries exist between what is perceived as work and play. For example, homework is perceived to have a low status among pupils:

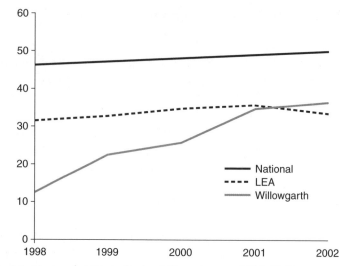

Figure 9.1: National, LEA and school X attainment 1998–2002

> We come to school to learn. We've done our work at school, and worked
> hard. Why should we go home and have to do more? My dad says I should
> get my work done during the day so I can have a laugh and play football
> after school. (Y9 student)

Staff at all levels perceive low expectations within the community as a
major barrier to progress:

> Lack of aspiration in the home. We have some children from some families
> that aren't engaged very effectively or educationally over a couple of
> generations or so. (headteacher)

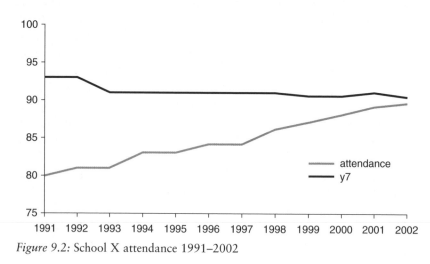

Figure 9.2: School X attendance 1991–2002

> You've got a lot of families where the kids don't get support. The parent's haven't been to higher education, they've not got jobs. The kids think they should be out every evening. (middle manager)

> A lot of pupils are not thinking about going onto higher education so there is not the natural motivation to study … A lot of them are aiming for local jobs around … A lot of them want to work for their dad and that is their ambition and that is what happens. (classroom teacher)

Historically, low expectations of staff were an issue, but staff do not exhibit low expectations now. They accept the attitudes and beliefs of the community are a significant barrier to improvement and understand that it is very hard to penetrate and mould the community's attitudes and beliefs to those of the school although this has been an area of progress in recent years:

> We're making great inroads into the community. So our relationships with parents have improved dramatically over the last six years but a lack of aspiration in the home persists. (headteacher)

Presenting issues

Examination of documentary evidence and interviews with staff highlighted four key issues. Each of these issues originated either from within the school or from beyond the school – although some occasions originated from a combination of both.

1 Inadequate resources

The perception is that historically this school was under-resourced by central government and the local education authority. Most interviewees linked increased resources to initiatives put in place after the election of New Labour in 1997:

> They [resources] have been a problem but that has eased a little over the past few years. (headteacher)
> For a long period until we joined the EAZ the problem was under-funding … The EAZ came along and back rolled us for three or four years. (senior manager)

Staff at all levels highlighted the importance of being part of an Education Action Zone (EAZ) initiative. Stating that first, it had provided important resources for the school that facilitated engagement in improvement-centred activity and, second, that it provided the focus for the activity; exploring teaching and learning with other schools in the zone. This EAZ is an example of a centrally conceived external intervention that met local expectations and needs. However, some interviewees recognized that in some ways the EAZ had served its purpose and now the school had moved to a position where another genre of intervention would be more appropriate.

2 Teaching and learning

The quality of teaching and learning within the school was an issue (Ofsted, 2003). Some interviewees reported that in the past teaching repertoires were limited and some teachers taught for control using mainly didactic approaches coupled with engaging the students in individual written work (copying activity, gap filling, etc.). The quality of teaching and learning was further compounded by the difficulties in recruiting and retaining highly motivated teachers, therefore having a further negative impact on the quality of teaching and learning.

3 Expectations

Historically, low expectations prevailed within and beyond School X. Interviewees within the school reported this to be the situation among most stakeholders, ranging from parents and the wider community, to teachers and the students themselves. It is likely that the turbulent socio-political and socio-economic context the community and the school had experienced during the last two decades have been important contributory factors towards this situation.

4 Prior attainment

Students had always entered the school with very low levels of prior attainment and still continue to do so. Low-prior attainment is widely recognized as one of the most reliable indicators of future academic performance (Teddlie and Reynolds, 2000). Therefore, the implications for school improvement are significant. To raise attainment and therefore examination performance of students in School X must be a particularly demanding challenge because of the characteristics of the cohort on entry.

The combination of the four presenting issues outlined above had a significant impact on the school. It is possible that the unique combination of these factors within such a fragile context had led to a situation that was self-perpetuating, creating a cycle where school improvement processes could not evolve. It was only when the leadership of the school (supported by favourable external conditions) specifically addressed these issues that the conditions evolved to enable the school to move forward.

An approach to school improvement

During the past five years School X has developed an overarching approach to improvement underpinned by several key principles:

- Investing in leadership at all levels.
- Developing secure structures to support teachers' work.
- Focusing on teaching and learning.
- Providing an appropriate curriculum.

Investing in leadership at all levels

Ofsted judged the leadership of the school as 'very good' in 2003. The style of the headteacher is high profile and perceived to be effective, often relying on traditional approaches and structures:

> You are the leader. I've heard people say that they do it all by delegation and so and so forth. But there are times when your staff need to know this is the problem and here I am in the front, I'm not lingering behind at the back, I'm at the front and this is what I think about it and this is what I propose to do about it. (headteacher)

However, the headteacher recognizes the importance of sharing leadership by releasing people's talents, abilities and opinions and dispersing leadership within a framework where staff have high levels of confidence in the headteacher:

> After that everybody leads. When I'm teaching [subject X] I'm a member of that department ... Once people know you've got the muscle for the job and you've got the stomach and vision for the job. You actually lead successfully by employing other people's talent, abilities and opinions, so I think the two [holding and devolving] have to go together ... You need to know when to be Head and you need to know when to be a colleague. (headteacher)

Developing secure structures to support teachers' work

Within this approach to school improvement the senior team have consciously focused on creating a purposeful learning environment. This has involved ensuring the arrangements at whole-school and departmental level support effective teaching and learning. Therefore, there are clear systems and policies in place, and they are reviewed and updated on a regular basis to reflect the changing needs of staff and students. Staff at all levels reported the importance of the clear behaviour management system:

> We've got very well established systems for managing pupil behaviour and promoting positive responses from pupils. Which I think is particularly important. (headteacher)

All levels of teachers also recognized the close relationship between good quality teaching and good discipline. Therefore, a central theme in all interviews was the unrelenting focus on improving teaching and learning.

> You can't separate them [teaching and discipline] they come together. You can't have effective teaching and learning if you don't have the discipline and you can't get the discipline without effective teaching. (classroom teacher)

Focusing on teaching and learning

The parallel approach of improving structures to support teaching and learning combined with improving the quality teaching and learning itself has led to a radical developments in pedagogy. Lessons have moved from a situation where 'teaching for control' was commonplace with teachers using didactic methods including copying from texts to ensure the appearance of an orderly, structured learning environment to a situation where teachers are experimenting and taking risks in their classrooms. Teachers have made efforts to broaden their teaching repertoire by taking advantage of continuing professional development activities, and have introduced new methods of teaching including incorporating multiple intelligence theory into their lessons to take learning styles of students into account. As a senior manager states:

> The important thing is not that we've stopped copying but that we are talking about education and the way people learn. (senior manager)

Providing an appropriate curriculum

In addition to improving the quality of teaching, the school's commitment to vocational education has also become valued by central government. The school has valued and developed vocational education for students over the last twenty years. Teachers are clear that their involvement in this area is not based on 'playing examination games' to get better GCSE scores through GNVQs. Rather, it is viewed as a long-term commitment to 'providing appropriate and stimulating curriculum experiences matched to student's needs'. Therefore, the school believes it is now getting recognized for work in this area that previously had eluded them.

Strategies for improvement

Within the approach to improvement briefly outlined above the school has implemented a complex range of complementary strategies that have successfully impacted on the four major presenting issues. This section describes examples of strategies employed within four key areas that have been central to the improvement of School X:

- Managing strategic improvement – the school development plan
- Cultural architecture – formation of express groups
- Creating a professional learning community – continuing professional development
- Breaking down barriers – the home–school partnership.

Managing strategic improvement – the school development plan

The senior team highlighted the importance of the school development plan. This was not viewed as a rhetorical document but as the 'coordinator' of improvement efforts that 'tied every thing together'. In reality the school development plan had been used to achieve coherence within the school's improvement efforts. This had minimized the extent that initiatives competed for resources within the school thus creating an improvement synergy that many schools (especially, those facing challenging circumstances) lack because disparate initiatives and interventions compete against each other, which at best cancel each other out and at worst have a negative effect.

The school development plan was not radical or spectacular in its design; rather it was clear, concise and focused on individual, team and whole-school outcomes based on improving teaching and learning. The plan was made through a combination of bottom-up and top-down approaches, therefore involvement and ownership was considered to be high. Each level within the plan was linked and resources, targets, success criteria and responsibilities were clearly outlined. Within the plan, monitoring and evaluation activity and responsibilities were clearly identified and time frames were indicated. There was provision for regular progress and success checks with senior and middle-level leaders, with the expectation that outcomes from these checks would be shared within departments at departmental meetings therefore involvement was inclusive. Senior team members considered the plan to be an *aide memoir* that could be used to assess progress towards achieving the aims, objectives and, ultimately, the vision of the school.

Cultural architecture – formation of express groups

All those interviewed spoke in very positive terms about the importance of express groups in moulding school culture and raising attainment. The number of students in express groups throughout the school has now risen to approximately 40 per cent. Express groups are mixed-ability tutorial groups selected on attitude. Individuals are selected for these groups in Year 7 and there is some movement in and out of them over the school year in each year group. Selection criteria are based on student attitude and commitment to school. Membership to an express group involves a number of rewards and additional commitment to school above what would be normally expected. For example, students in express groups have a longer school day, higher attendance targets, they are often entered early for public examinations (especially maths) and have increased access to the best facilities available within the school (especially ICT). Express groups have created a 'can do' culture where learning is perceived to be 'cool'. In addition to supporting the development of a positive culture, express groups have also raised the expectations of both students and staff. Success has become infectious as students see their peers achieve and get rewarded and teachers witness students achieving results previously thought unattainable. This situation has led to an ongoing readjustment of what is considered possible within the school. Raised expectations have led to competition to get in to an express group. Students interviewed that were not part of express groups were keen to join one, however, they did not appear to feel excluded, resentful or jealous of peers who were already part of an express group.

Creating a professional learning community – continuing professional development

One of the central presenting issues for School X was the quality of teaching and learning. In an attempt to raise the quality in these areas the school has supported the professional development of staff. Although this has involved some formal lesson observation for the purposes of performance management etc., this type of formal observation (much to the irritation of the LEA and unlike many other schools facing challenging circumstances) has, where possible, been avoided. The senior leaders do not view this mode of lesson observation as developmental and would prefer to monitor classroom teaching on a more informal basis by walking around the school. Teachers and departments have engaged in professional development activity in a number of ways. First, there have been some external speakers invited into the school to talk about topics related to teaching and learning. The success of these sessions has relied on high-quality presentation from the speaker resulting in staff discussing aspects of teaching and learning. Out of these discussions a common discourse has developed pertaining to teaching and learning. Second, the EAZ has provided the opportunity for teachers to share ideas and good practice between each other within the school and also within departmental groups across schools. Third, teachers also plan collaboratively on an informal basis and regularly share resources and teaching 'tips'. It appears that most peer-observation and team-teaching occur on an informal basis within departments. Fourth, where possible teachers are encouraged to take on extra responsibilities to broaden their professional knowledge and skills. The majority of these opportunities appear to be linked directly to teaching or leadership responsibilities rather than administrative responsibilities. Where possible the leadership group supports these appointments with incremental pay points. The school acknowledges there is much progress to be made in this area and it is in its infancy in terms of developing a professional learning community. However, it is proud of the progress made from a very low base line.

Breaking down barriers – home–school partnership

As previously noted, community expectations were also low and it is likely that many parents/carers would themselves have had negative experiences of school. The school has taken deliberate steps to make positive contact with parents. For example, positive telephone calls or praise postcards were often sent in recognition of good conduct/ progress etc. Also adults were welcomed into the school in an attempt to break down the negative feelings associated with their own previous experiences. A particularly interesting development was the introduction of a new format to parents evening. The traditional parents evening was discontinued and a 'parents' week' was introduced. It became the responsibility of the form tutor to make a home contact, initially by phone or letter to each of the parents/carers of students in their tutor group. During this conversation an appointment was made for the parents to meet with the form tutor to discuss the student's progress in all subjects. Only if there were severe concerns or need for high levels of praise would the parents discuss this with the subject teacher during 'parents' week'. If no appointment could be arranged or the appointment was subsequently missed, then another phone call was made and the discussion conducted over the telephone. This change in routines contributed to the school raising home–school contact levels during parents' evenings from just over 30 per cent to over 95 per cent in 'parents' week'.

The four areas outlined above and the strategies contained within them represent practical approaches to school improvement in a particular context. However, it must be recognized that, first, this case can only portray a simplistic version of the complex reality of improving of a social organization. Second, and perhaps most importantly, without the energetic effective and experienced leadership of the senior team combined with an ever-increasingly strong group of middle-level leaders the improvements made at this school may have been impossible to attain within this demanding context or within so short a time frame.

Teachers within the school were proud to highlight the successes but they also understood the complexity and fragility of improving schools in challenging contexts. The drive for sustaining improvements was central to the leadership's existence. Teachers at all levels were continuously seeking new ideas from outside the school and were willing to experiment with them in their own classrooms.

Commentary

A number of tensions have emerged as School X progressed. These tensions have implications for other schools in challenging contexts, and possibly beyond. Two tensions that came to the fore in this case were related directly to the national landscape but also compounded by the nature of the challenging context. First, it is clear that School X has been flexible in its operational procedures especially relating to curriculum. However, the school has had the strength of leadership and the confidence to take risks. Many schools in challenging contexts may not possess these attributes and may feel less confident in challenging what is currently a prescriptive narrow curriculum where success or failure is judged on narrow academic outcomes. Schools in the most challenging circumstances that are serving the most challenging communities must be given the flexibility to experiment with alternative curricula pathways based on broader success criteria. The implementation of the 14–19 curriculum may go some way to making this possible. However, whether it will provide equity across the system that ensures appropriate experiences for all children remains questionable.

Second, it is widely recognized that recruitment and retention of staff is a national issue. In low-attaining schools or schools that serve particularly difficult communities it is unsurprising that the recruitment and retention of appropriate teachers remains problematic. Some schools are trapped in a situation where large numbers of vacancies have to be filled with short-term supply staff or temporary teachers from overseas.

This situation is likely to create a scenario where collaborative cultures quickly fragment and the quality of teaching drops. This in turn may lead to student disaffection and indiscipline, which in turn will further fragment the culture and thus the cycle is likely to be repeated. Therefore, the recruitment and, perhaps more importantly, the retention of teachers is paramount to success.

School X has been creative in the way that it has recruited teachers. The school actively plans for succession of staff. Talent spotting from cohorts of PGCE students on teaching practice is commonplace. The school also engages in proactive recruitment, using extended networks within and beyond the LEA to identify the best candidates for advertised posts. On successful recruitment of teachers, the school takes care to nurture, respect and motivate them through comprehensive professional development programmes and the provision of wider leadership opportunities. Ironically, this strategy has resulted in supporting continued staff turnover. However, staff now leave the school for promotion to other schools rather than hoping to move to a less challenging environment. Consequently, the reputation of School X has improved and teachers are attracted to the school because they view employment there as a pathway to development and promotion. Thus, an upward momentum is created and sustained with a constant (albeit modest) flow of motivated teachers entering the school offsetting the loss of those to promoted positions.

In conclusion, School X is a school where teachers want to teach and students want to learn. The leadership and staff of the school have created whole-school and classroom conditions that support teaching and learning. Therefore, over time disaffection of students has been reduced and discipline and student experiences improved. Teachers are willing to work in this challenging environment because, first, they feel supported by their colleagues and, second, they believe with good quality teaching and learning they can make a difference to the lives of the students they teach. Therefore, the emotional and value-based dimensions of school improvement can not be underestimated. This suggests that schools in challenging contexts that neglect the emotional dimensions of school improvement in favour of adherence to simplistic technical-rational approaches are likely to fail to engage in genuine sustainable school improvement. However, the caveat 'Let's be realistic' (Thrupp, 1999) must also be recognized. Schools and classrooms only account for up to 20 per cent variance in achievement, the rest being attributed to other factors such as individual pupil factors including parental socio-economic status (Teddlie and Reynolds, 2000). Therefore, the context within which these schools operate must be accepted as an explanation rather than an excuse for unremarkable results in crude examination performance.

Note

1 For definition see Reynolds, *et al.* (2001).

References

Barber, M. and Dann, R. (1996) *Raising Educational Standards in the Inner Cities.* London: Cassell.

Elmore, R. (2000) *Building a New Structure for School Leadership.* Washington, DC: Albert Shanker Institute.

Evans, R. L. and Teddlie, C. (1995) 'Facilitating change in schools: is there one best style?', *School Effectiveness and School Improvement*, 6, 1, 1–22.

Gore, T. and Smith, N. (2001) *Patterns of Educational Attainment in the British Coalfields.* London: DfES.

Gray, J. (2000) *Causing Concern but Improving.* London: Department for Education and Skills.

Hallinger, P. and Murphy, J. (1986) 'The social context of effective schools', *The American Journal of Education*, 94, 328–55.

Hargreaves. D. H. (1997) 'School culture, school effectiveness and school improvement', reprinted in Harris, A., Bennett, N. and Preedy, M. (eds) *Organizational Effectiveness and Improvement in Education*, Buckingham: Open University Press.

Harris, A., Muijs, D., Chapman, C., Stoll, L. and Russ, J. (2003) *Raising Attainment in Former Coalfield Areas.* Sheffield: DfES.

Hopkins, D. (2001a) *Meeting the Challenge: An Improvement Guide for Schools Facing Challenging Circumstances.* London: DfEE.

Hopkins, D. (2001b) *School Improvement for Real.* London: Routledge.

Hopkins, D., Harris, A. and Jackson, D. (1997) 'Understanding a school's capacity for development: growth states and strategies', *School Leadership and Management*, 17, 3, 401–11.

Louis, K. and Miles, M. B. (1990) *Improving the Urban High School: What Works and Why?* New York: Teachers College Press.

Louis, K. and Marks, H. (1996) 'Teachers' professional community in restructuring schools', *American Educational Research Journal*, 33, 4, 757–89.

Maden, M. (2001) *Further Lessons in Success. Success Against the Odds – Five Years On.* London, Routledge Falmer.

National Commission on Education (1996) *Success Against the Odds: Effective Schools in Disadvantaged Areas.* London: Routledge.

Ofsted (2003) *Inspection Report School X.* London: Ofsted.

Reynolds, D., Hopkins, D., Potter, D. and Chapman, C. (2001) *School Improvement in Schools Facing Challenging Circumstances: A Review of Research and Practice*. London: DfEE.

Rozenholtz, S. J. (1989) *Teachers' Workplace: The Social Organization of Schools*. New York: Longman.

Rutter, M., Maughan, B., Mortimore, P. and Ouston, J. (1979) *Fifteen Thousand Hours: Secondary Schools and Their Effects on Children*. London: Open Books.

Sammons, P., Thomas, S. and Mortimore, P. (1997) *Forging Links: Effective Schools and Effective Departments*. London: Chapman.

Sammons, P. (1999) *School Effectiveness: Coming of Age in the Twenty-First Century*. Lisse: Swets and Zeitlinger

Stoll, L. and Myers, K. (1998) *No Quick Fixes: Perspectives on Schools in Difficulty*. London: Falmer

Stoll, L. and Fink, D. (1996) *Improving our Schools*. Buckingham: Open University Press.

Thrupp, M. (1999) *Schools Make a Difference: Let's be Realistic!* Buckingham: Open University Press.

Teddlie, C. and Reynolds, D. (2000) *The International Handbook of School Effectiveness Research*. London: Falmer.

Teddlie, C. and Stringfield, S. (1993) *School Matters: Lessons Learned from a 10-Year Study of School Effects*. New York: Teachers College Press.

Endpiece: Legitimacy and Action

Paul Clarke

> The more the state intervenes in seeking to provide rational, technical and scientific administrative solutions, the more it is required to listen to and acknowledge the cultural norms and interests of widely disparate groups and, concomitantly, the greater the risk it runs of losing credibility because of its ultimate inability to deliver promised solutions in a situation of complex decision overload. (Habermas, 1976)

Purposeful improvement to legitimize change

As modern industrial societies have in recent years grappled with the challenges of economic and social dislocation, educational change has been seen increasingly as a major feature of regenerative activity. Many centralized initiatives spawned under the school improvement agenda have been little more than tinkering at the edges of a 'stuck' system (Rosenholtz 1989)[1] in that they have failed to generate the local sense of need for meaningful change (Clarke, 2000; Wrigley, 2003; Riddell, 2003). Whilst there is plenty of evidence of centralized effort to influence practice at classroom, management and network[2] levels to ensure sustained impact of policy, the strategy has tended to isolate each effort, rather than integrate them as a conceptual whole to generate a strategic approach which grapples with the complexities of that whole. The sum of this approach is the feeling of fragmentation of people's work lives, of their professional role and of their individual and shared capability to make real sense of the situations in which they work (Sennett, 1998). In such circumstances people can become increasingly disillusioned and feel disempowered. The consequent effect of this is the possibility of mass withdrawal of support – a crisis of legitimacy.

This atomization of policy into a series of manageable, budget-driven programmes is a predictable approach from the governmental centre; it enables each strand of activity aimed at each level of the system to be thoroughly audited and monitored. However, it is destined to fail simply because it is based on a premise of conceptual coherence and progressive and consistent uptake by implementer teachers. Basically, it assumes a logical response at the school. As we have seen in this book, headteachers, teachers and support staff operate inside schools which are seen as static receivers of externally defined and formulated policy (Sarason, 1990). It illustrates a way of thinking about change which is widespread, embedded systemically and, I suggest, wholly inappropriate for the type of challenges which our schools now face whether they be in difficulty or not. Put simply, our schools are not logical places, they are vibrant emotional jungles of contested views, emergent ideas, with pockets of fully or partially formed strategies that are in a state of constant flux because of the circumstances in which they are located. The status quo, evident as a set response to a highly complex social network of the school, is no longer an adequately fashioned model.

These days, at the core of the ideology of improving schools lies an ideology of managerialism. Mangerialism pursues the notion that all aspects of educational development can improve the quality of learning simply through the betterment of managed and aligned systems. Government education policies across centralized education systems in the developed world overwhelmingly emphasize managerial change and increased school accountability (Townsend *et al.*, 1999). Whilst reforms attend to structural needs, they fail to make any real sense of an integrated approach inside a dynamic cultural environment.

Here lies the main problem. It is a problem which has been examined by my colleagues in various ways in the chapters of this book. Namely, it is not possible to fashion and mandate a strategic programme of intervention with schools that engages with their needs emotionally as well as practically and that galvanizes action and then sustains local support in such a way as to change behaviour for the longer term. The implication of assuming otherwise is that our communities are monocultural, anodyne and static, which they plainly are not. We live in communities which are diverse, disparate and nuanced, they are dynamic environments and, as such, the likelihood of a central system meeting the needs of such places within a democratic society are extremely limited to a set of reductive, blunt instruments of change. As these communities become more sophisticated and interconnected, the distance becomes greater between their endeavours to sustain educational support and any effort to define and manage this from a centralized position.

This interface, between educational change at a local level and economic rationalism as an ideology of educational change from the centre, does not fit together neatly. The most visible signs of its weakness are to be found in locations where the benefits of economic development have had the least effect. This is usually where our schools in difficulty are located. Over 30 years of research has consistently demonstrated that academic achievement in schools is closely correlated with student socio-economic status (Anyon, 1997) as well as individual aspiration, a point reinforced in this book by many of my colleagues.

I maintain that to really improve poorer children's life chances, in school and out, we should look towards trying to increase their social and economic well-being, status and ambition. In order to eliminate poverty and enhance aspiration, society must eliminate the school in challenging circumstances by eliminating the underlying causes of challenge and offer a new sense of hope and possibility. We, of course, celebrate small victories such as the restructuring of a school or the introduction of a new classroom teaching technique, but we must not delude ourselves, these small victories cannot add up to large victories with effects that are sustainable unless they are coupled with long-range systemic strategy. This strategy needs to be geared to eradicate underlying causes of poverty and racial isolation, as well as being geared to enhance the sense of personal and collective agency. Circumstances of extreme challenge demand the fusion of local support as well as that from further afield. The problem is how to do this without resorting to a strategic approach which reduces the disparate elements of the challenge into small manageable chunks because, in so doing, the essence of the problem is so often lost and as a result we witness governments resorting to ever more technical and technicized efforts to improve schools. Such efforts fail because they alienate, they devolve power away from school towards the externally defined solution and, as such, they lose internal legitimacy. To lose within school legitimacy is to lose credibility with the users or implementers (Clarke, 2001; Codd, 1999; Betts *et al.*, 2002; Mintzberg, 1994), those very people charged with implementing the changes, i.e., the teachers. What perhaps begins as good intention ends up as a reductive, awkward and overly beauracratic requirement, something that is 'done-to' teachers, rather than 'done-with' them.

In part this response by teachers can be accused of being is ill-informed, as it fails to grasp the wider based imperatives associated with economic rationalism and the managed market of education (Marginson, 1993; Pusey, 1991) but in the resistance there is another understanding which is being voiced which connects closely to what makes educational change embed, namely the authenticity of context and local cultural nuance – *change that matters to the people making the changes*. This connection is very important. It recognizes that teaching in school is essentially about human relationships, and in places of difficulty the moral purpose of the teacher is very often about enhancing the life chances of students through those relationships. An overdependence on 'fixes', be they short or long-term, takes insufficient account of how to empower implementers to become formulators of their own strategic designs inside their own communities in ways that are persuasive (Mintzberg, 1994). There is, therefore, a logic to resistance at the local level, to policy which seemingly fails to connect to local circumstance on human, and not economic terms. It is the logic of local know-how, local culture and local community, and we should learn from it if we are to improve the ways we work with schools in difficulty.

If we are to begin to offer a way forward, we face a structural challenge. Despite many years of effort to overcome school difficulty, it is still the case that many schools in challenging circumstances are victims of fragmented, isolationist and narrow strategic goal setting for externally defined developments which reproduce rather than transform the existing social inequalities.

> Competition, choice, and performance indicators remain the unchallenged totems of policy, not in overt policy statements but simply by being left untouched by the New Labour reforms. Structurally, little that is fundamental is changing in the ways in which schools and colleges are run. Markets and managerialism hold sway. Structures and methods remain largely unaltered. (Fergusson, 2000: 203)

We do not, regretfully, have a system which regularly opens schools for visiting teachers to observe, share findings and report back to their own colleagues as described by Ainscow and colleagues in Chapter 7. Our organizational structures within and between schools by and large remain locked to the Victorian era of isolated classroom units and individualized classes designated to single teachers. To compensate somewhat for this disgraceful paucity of organizational innovation, and to tackle the ever-increasing frustrations of students and many staff, an extension of the managerial approach from the structures of the school is being imported to the classroom. The learning process itself is now been subjected to similarly reductive interpretations in an effort to maintain social order. It will not work, and will unfortunately have the opposite effect to that which it maintains to promote – less creative and less empowered teachers, and a set of more defined, less engaged learners who are subjected to someone else's curriculum which represents a very distant world view far from that which they know, experience and care about.

Over the last few years we have seen successive governments intervene ever more upon the classroom, so that the national curriculum is no longer a guide on 'what' to teach, but with the addition of the literacy and numeracy hours the reform becomes focused on 'how' to teach in order to improve student and teacher performance. Alongside these efforts come performance management strategies because it is absolutely necessary, having initiated such a system, that teachers charged with implementing the work are carrying it through. As Thrupp and Wilmott (2003) argue, this type of government intervention is paradoxical. It is at once seen as expansive, opening up a whole new way of looking at schooling through 'modernization' aimed at improved performance of the managed system, with a sharpness of focus on performance management, and yet it is also limited to the extent that performance management focuses school leadership on to the core tasks of enhancing pupil progress against a set of measurable outcomes (ibid: 31).

It seems to me, having explored this ground many times with colleagues in difficult schools, that, at best, the outside-in approach to reform will provide a starting point. But once it begins, there has to be a much better basis for its support to legitimize it if ideas and new insights are to flourish (Sergiovanni, 1992). To do this we have to first encourage the school to become more introspective and self-reflective, whilst at the same time putting teams of teachers[3] together in forums where they can meet with a wider range of opinions and teaching styles, through which they can open the dialogue of change and development – as Judith Warren-Little once remarked so that 'teachers teach each other the practice of teaching'. This simple yet effective approach serves to internalize a real dialogue on the conditions, the challenges and the possibilities that the community of people within the school feel that they most wish to engage.

Reconstructing the discourse of change

What I am leading to is that we face a difficult time working with difficult schools. This is because we are slowly learning that the ways which might best suit their needs are not the ways at the moment that are highly valued by the existing system. They may, incidentally, show signs of short-term improvement in performance, but will this will not transfer into longer-term renewal and regeneration under existing arrangements. As Leadbeater (1999) tells us, we have a nineteenth-century school organizational model full of twenty-first century people.

> We have not yet created new institutions of co-operation and collective endeavour, to protect us against new risks, to share the rewards and to match the pace of innovation and knowledge creation (Leadbeater, 1999: 54)

If we are to ask teachers to take on much bigger, more complex changes to achieve significant improvement, it is inevitable that we will see an increase in the levels of failure. People will blunder, they will struggle with new ideas and what they do will look clumsy and sometimes ill-conceived, but it will be theirs, and will be drawn from their lived experience, it will have integrity and ownership. Our existing system does not tolerate failure, built as it was on mechanistic and incremental models of learning and organization for the factory era. However, to move forward, our school leaders must learn how to maximize the potential for success just as so many have learnt how to minimize the opportunity to fail under existing structures. To do this they need to be offered ways of reinterpreting the process of growth in their own school settings and to then have the operational freedom to explore and experiment with their approaches.

It is to this issue that I will now turn. I wanted at the end of the book to illustrate just one way that we are playing with these ideas arising from our work with schools in difficulty in the IQEA programme and through the Octet programme. In Chapter 1 we described a three-phase process which we were using as we modelled our developmental activity with schools in extremely challenging circumstances drawn from the experiences of working in IQEA and the High Reliability Schools Programme.

If the locus for real educational reform is the interface between teacher and learner, then we are trying to change this relationship, this experience, and this opportunity for learning, and at least three significant dimensions of change need to be simultaneously enhanced:

- Personal learning, in the attitudinal shift required of the teacher and the learner to accommodate new ways of working – this is an emotional as well as a practical matter asking: who am I in this situation?
- Cultural learning, in the systemic development which pervades the entire school environment, this is an organizational as well as an individual matter asking who are we and what are we trying to do here.
- Pedagogic learning, which necessitates a move away from centrally mandated 'technical' solutions towards a deeper and more personalized form of learning about teaching. This is where the professional teacher is encouraged to participate in direct and meaningful investigation into his/her own practice with students and close-working colleagues asking 'why do I teach like this?'

In each of these cases, the human scale or 'second-order' development is a vital ingredient to the success of the reform; these types of exchanges are more complex and reciprocal in kind and reflect much more closely the types of exchanges which arise daily inside schools. As Mulgan (1998) observes,

The Market system has become phenomenally sophisticated at managing what could be called first-order exchanges – like buying a car, a loaf of bread or a television set, in which it is unnecessary to have any continuing relationship with the partner of exchange. But it is less sophisticated at second-order exchanges which, like most human relationships, depend upon reciprocal understandings.

It is these reciprocal understandings which seem to me to be the foundation for new work in schools in difficulty if we are to engage in a new era of learning schools within a learning system. They arise through enhanced interaction between, in this case, teachers talking about their own teaching experiences – we deliberately seek to enhance the social and intellectual capital of self and organization and we do this through the simple tool of dialogue.

It is Michael Fielding who steadfastly maintains that there is an urgent need to rediscover the power of real dialogue between teachers and students (Fielding, 1999) – to achieve this is not an easy option. It seems necessary and appropriate to encourage all participants in school (teachers and students) to engage in reflection on their work and to identify aspects of their work that they feel have some meaning and relevance to them and their situation. In so doing, a learner begins to construct an opinion of her own practice and is in a position to talk about that practice with a colleague, from her own class, her school or elsewhere. This begins a process of reciprocal understanding, where description, observation and modeling stimulate new insights and possibilities for development amongst individuals.

Having begun a conversation based on her own practice, the learner returns to her own classroom and takes forward some of the discussion in the form of modified learning activity. At this point a structural issue comes in to play which is very important for the potential of the whole process. Historically, in such a cycle of activity, the learner might return to the earlier stage in the cycle and discuss this work further with a colleague or peer. In our recent work, we have observed and subsequently encouraged a modification to this process, where the learner returns to a larger group and connects her work to that of her colleagues, from which they discuss in more depth the factors which seem to enable progress and the factors which seem to inhibit progress (Clarke *et al.*, 2005). This often most-fruitful dialogue moves the team forward, where they are exploring the deeper meaning behind their actions and critically identifying matters which need to be overcome if they are to proceed to their satisfaction. A final stage in this part of the process sees the formation of teams. Note that this happens quite some time into the discussions and is not formally established at the start of any cycle of discussion. We have found that the evolution of the teams works much better than the predefined groupings, so teams ebb and flow according to the interest and need, but they are expected to remain open and not an exclusive club within school – in effect, classes evolve as a result of the discussions.

Having generated teams who begin to work on shared areas of enquiry, we see a third phase of what we call 'co-creating of learning' taking place. Here, new 'prototype' strategies for classroom learning are explored within a secure collegial environment. These real-world experiences hold considerable value for the teachers and students. They are embedded in their own shared experience. They reflect efforts to enhance a specific aspect of practice which has itself been identified as significant in their classroom or as work needed to be improved in order to have a significant influence on the lives of their students. The outcome of this reflective work leads to the teams presenting their practical accomplishments to other teams, perhaps from the same class, or from parallel classes, or from other parts of school, or perhaps from other schools who are working in their network or local community of schools. This end point in phase three provides a point at which new people can join in phase one and be introduced to experiences and examples from their colleagues. It also allows for the more experienced colleagues in established teams to begin to spawn new links with new thematic activity.

Throughout this one process, with its three phases and a series of developmental steps, it is possible to see teams of learners, as well as individuals, loop back into earlier iterations of their discussions as well as jumping forward and anticipating new approaches and opportunities. What I have tried to describe here is a dynamic process of learning, which offers a practical way forward for colleagues engaged in activity which seeks to engage the learner deeply inside her lived experience and, from this, to draw out facets of practice which allow for personal and organizational growth.

This process of reciprocal meaning-making is very powerful, particularly in schools in difficulty, because it opens the possibility for creativity. It is located inside a field of activity where teachers and learners have direct influence and authority. It legitimizes their personal interests and passions relating to the experience of learning in their school community.

Our experience of working in difficult schools, captured in different facets and stories in this book, suggests that it is vital to create space for all learners to generate deep levels of trust and support for each other if they are to engage meaningfully in their educational journey. The community of the school is not a snappy label to be slapped on the front of the school magazine, it is a critical tool which needs to be nurtured, exposed, challenged and redefined by its participants – there is much that is yet to be learnt about how we might proceed, but one thing which we do know, and as yet do not value, is the power of critical dialogue.

Notes

1 I use the term 'stuck' to refer to the school system in a similar way to that which Susan Rosenholtz first used the term to describe schools as either stuck or moving (Rosenholtz, 1989).
2 For example, literacy and numeracy strategies, middle management training, leadership incentive grants, networked learning communities, etc.
3 I recognize that I am emphasizing teacher development here as a first step. It is quite possible I think, to pursue the same agenda with students, where the circumstances suit doing that. My recent experience has been with a very specific group of schools in extreme challenge, our remit was very focused on teacher and classroom development and, as a result, my reflections in this chapter relate to that experience.

References

Anyon, J. (1997) *Ghetto Schooling: A Political Economy of Urban Education Reform*. London. Teachers College Press.

Betts, J., Clegg, S. and Clarke, P. (2002) 'The discourse of success and failure in organizational learning'. *International Journal of Human Resources Development and Management*, 2, 1/2, 97–112.

Clarke, P. (2000) *Learning Schools, Learning Systems*. London: Continuum.

Clarke, P. (2001) 'Feeling compromised – the impact on teachers of the performance culture', *Improving Schools*, 4, 3.

Codd, J. (1999) 'Educational reform, accountability and the culture of distrust', in Thrupp, M. (ed.) *A Decade of Reform in New Zealand Education: Where to Now?* Waikato, NZ: University of Waikato.

Fergusson, R. (2000) 'Modernising managerialism in education', in J. Clarke, S. Gewirtz and E. McLaughlin (eds) *New Managerialism, New Welfare?* London: Sage.

Fielding, M. (ed.) (2001) *Taking Education Really Seriously: Four Years Hard Labour*. London: Routledge Falmer.

Habermas, J. *Legitimation Crisis*. (1976) Trans. T. McCarthy. London: Polity Press.

Leadbeater, C. (1999) *Living on Thin Air*. London: Penguin Books.

Marginson, S. (1993) *Education and Policy in Australia*. Cambridge: Cambridge University Press.

Mintzberg, H. (1994) *The Rise and Fall of Strategic Planning*. New York: The Free Press.

Mulgan, G. (1998) *Connexity: How to Live in a Connected World*. Cambridge, MA: Harvard Business School Press.

Pusey, M. (1991) *Economic Rationalism in Canberra*. Cambridge: Cambridge University Press.

Riddell, R. (2003) *Schools for our Cities: Urban Learning in the 21st Century*. Stoke-on-Trent: Trentham Books.

Rosenholtz, S. J. (1989) *Teachers' Workplace: The Social Organization of Schools*. London: Longman.

Sarason, S. B. (1990) *The Predictable Failure of Educational Reform: Can We Change Course Before It's Too Late?* San Francisco: Jossey-Bass.

Sennett, R. (1998) *The Corrosion of Character: Personal Consequences of Work in the New Capitalism*. London: W. W. Norton & Company Ltd.

Sergiovanni, T. (1992) *Moral Leadership: Getting to the Heart of School Improvement*. San Francisco: Jossey-Bass.

Thrupp, M. and Wilmott, R. (2003) *Education Management in Managerialist Times: Beyond the Textual Apologists*. Buckingham: Open University Press.

Townsend, T., Clarke, P. and Ainscow, M. (eds) (1999) *Third Millennium Schools: A World of Difference in Effectiveness and Improvement*. Rotterdam: Swets and Zeitlinger.

Wrigley, T. (2003) *Schools of Hope: A New Agenda for School Improvement*. Stoke-on-Trent: Trentham Books.

Index

An 'f' after a page number indicates inclusion of a figure; a 't' indicates inclusion of a table.